D0474694

FIVE VIEWS OF
MULTI-RACIAL BRITAIN

**Talks on race relations
broadcast by BBC TV**

Published by
Commission for Racial Equality
by special arrangement with
BBC Television Further Education

KA 0007609 0

KING ALFRED'S COLLEGE
WINCHESTER,

305.8
FIV

80157

Commission for Racial Equality
Elliot House
10-12 Allington Street
London SW1E 5EH
Telephone: 01-828 7022

©   The authors

First Edition
August, 1978

Second Edition
November, 1978

ISBN 0 902355 79 1

Note: This booklet contains the full text of five talks on race relations, extracts of which were first broadcast by the BBC TV in July, 1978.

Printed by Interlink Longraph Ltd. 45 Mitchell Street, London EC1.

Contents

Foreword

Too often, the media confuse 'race relations' with 'immigration'. To those working for good race relations in Britain, it seems that many journalists are pre-occupied with immigration and forget that it has already declined to a low level and that the fulfilment of our remaining obligations is more likely to assist integration in this country than damage it.

The repercussions of this distortion by the media are disturbing to those who recognise that Britain is now a multi-racial society and that its future development and well-being require the dispelling of fears and anxieties that arise from ignorance and prejudice.

I warmly welcome the BBC's initiative in giving a public platform to five of the most distinguished authorities on race relations in Britain and in enabling us to provide a permanent and full record of their talks. We at the Commission for Racial Equality do not necessarily share all the views they express; but we do recognise that our targets are the same — that is, the promotion of equal opportunity and the establishment of a harmonious multi-racial society in Britain.

To that end, we believe that the views expressed in this booklet deserve the widest consideration and debate.

David Lane
Chairman
Commission for Racial Equality

Introduction

John Twitchin, Producer, 'Multi-Racial Britain',
BBC Television Further Education Department

In broadcasting extracts from the public talks now reprinted in full in this booklet, the BBC aimed to make a contribution to a more rational and informed debate on questions of race relations in our society. But, it may be objected, why is this necessary?

Each year, the public is presented with a continual spate of news coverage of events which are plainly symptomatic of the general state of race relations in Britain. In the first six months of 1978 alone, for example, we've already seen recurrent political argument about possible further changes in immigration policy; there's been the all-party Select Committee Report on Immigration; there was a major demonstration by Asian Youth in protest against the killing of an Asian Bengalee in London's East End; there was the G.L.C. row over whether Asians would be safe from racist assaults if they were housed in what the press called 'ghettos'; and there are the constantly reported street-level activities of the National Front, now often countered by the demonstrations and rock carnivals involving the Anti-Nazi League.

The authors of these talks are among the many well-informed specialists who are worried that such events are signalling an overall worsening of race relations — despite the anti-discrimination legislation and the efforts, so far, of agencies like the CRE. Stuart Hall and Bhikhu Parekh are particularly concerned, too, to note a slippage, since the early '60s, in the language of public debate and opinion towards racist assumptions. As a result of their analysis all the authors point to a need for further changes in public policies — at parliamentary level and at local authority level — together with changes in priorities and training needs at workplaces, in schools, in public community services and, not least, in the media, if the direction of these trends is to be reversed.

Now many educated people, especially if they don't themselves live in an inner city area alongside ethnic minority groups, feel that this sort of talk is altogether too exaggerated. 'After all,' they argue, 'all societies have conflicts of interest and are subject to social pressures — so a degree of racial friction is only to be expected. The British have always been xenophobic about anyone from south, west or east of the English Channel — but history shows that despite initial strains, any immigrant group is absorbed within one to two generations. We and our friends are not colour prejudiced, and nobody else would be if the 'professional do-gooders' didn't keep drawing unnecessary attention to the problems temporarily faced by minority groups. And in any case, isn't 'positive discrimination' on behalf of any group little more than a plea for privilege, which will simply produce its own backlash?'

This sort of thinking, the 'colour blind eye' approach, was arguably justifiable in the 1950s, when there were few signs of friction. But these public talks make clear just why events since then make it no longer appropriate in facing the 1980s. The weight of evidence of discrimination and disadvantage experienced by the black minority*, together with the continuing tensions of the inner city areas, force the conclusion that more effective policies and forms of positive discrimination may now be needed if an escalation of tension is to be avoided. Unfortunately, there are grounds to suspect that this evidence remains largely ignored outside the circle of the 'race relations industry'. Perhaps the publicity work done by the race relations agencies is too easily set aside as special pleading. But the result of ignorance of the facts, rationalised by the 'leave well alone' approach, has been to leave the stage clear for those who, wittingly or otherwise, speak and act on racist assumptions to take the initiative both in opinion leadership and in setting the agenda of public discussion.

In a sense, therefore, these talks can be seen as part of an overdue attempt to provide some of the facts and theory needed for a better informed public discussion of race relations issues. Such issues can readily call into play all sorts of irrational emotions. This makes it all the more important that the debate be conducted on a firmer basis of argument than vague moral appeals to 'tolerance', or political rhetoric based on assumed short-term electoral advantage. And to the extent that it needs to be conducted in terms based more on facts than on generalisations derived impressionistically from the news media, these talks do much to supply that need. The authors have expert knowledge of race relations, based on sound academic researches. Their talks offer authoritative analytic tools for honestly confronting and thinking through some of the fundamental social questions on which our public policies are premised — for example, What are the preconditions for a multi-racial society to function successfully? What are the real causes of racial conflict and friction? Why are different cultural values felt as a 'threat'? How far does recurrent political debate about immigration policies serve to distract attention from questions about handling race relations in Britain, and hinder rather than help the education of public opinion about them?

*The evidence given in the Political and Economic Planning reports in particular is referred to by several of the authors. The key booklets are *The Facts of Racial Disadvantage* and *Racial Discrimination in Employment,* both by David J. Smith. Available from PEP, 12 Upper Belgrave Street, London SW1X 8BB.

What comes through in reading the talks by John Rex, Stuart Hall, and Alan Little, is not only that these questions are complex, and merit concentrated attention, but that such questions cannot be treated as matters of abstract argument alone. Real understanding of race relations requires a degree of imagination and sensitivity to the experience of ethnic minorities living in a society which still appears hostile, in so many ways, to them. The sensitivity required is much more than merely paternalist interest in minority group culture, and for many white English people who don't have occasion to get to know West Indians or Asians personally, it may not be easy to develop.

That is why we were so pleased to be able to include the talks by Bhikhu Parekh and by Trevor Huddleston. Dr Parekh may hardly be a 'typical' Asian Briton, but he offers some frank and moving insights into the Asian experience and perception of life here. Bishop Huddleston, too, in drawing our attention to the wider international implications of how we handle our race relations in Britain, speaks directly from a unique personal experience — of both the racist regime in South Africa and of the multi-racial society of Tanzania.

In selecting just five talks for the BBC series, perhaps the most important aspect of race relations that we've not covered is the field of race and employment. A note about this, together with details about how to obtain copies of the BBC films, appears on page 76.

Finally, I should like to take the opportunity to thank the five authors again for allowing us to film their public talks, and to thank the CRE and the staff of the Information Department, in particular, for the remarkable speed and energy with which they have made this booklet available.

The Contributors

Professor John Rex has been Professor of Sociology at the University of Warwick since 1970. Educated in South Africa, he lectured at the Universities of Leeds and Birmingham before becoming Professor of Social Theory and Institutions at Durham in 1964. He was Visiting Professor at Toronto in 1974-75. His publications include *Race Relations and Sociological Theory,* 1970; *Discovering Sociology,* 1973 and *Race, Colonialism and the City,* 1974.

Dr Stuart Hall was born in Jamaica. He won a Rhodes Scholarship and read English at Oxford. For two years he taught at a secondary school in Brixton and was editor of Universities and Left Review, and, later on the editorial committee of New Left Review. He was lecturer in liberal studies at the Chelsea College of Science from 1961-63 after which he became Research Fellow and later Director of the Centre for Contemporary Cultural Studies at the University of Birmingham.

Dr Bhikhu Parekh was born in India and came to Britain in 1959. After obtaining a Ph.D at the London School of Economics, he was a tutor there from 1961-62. Since 1964 Dr Parekh has been with the University of Hull, but has been a Visiting Professor to three North American universities. He is Chairman of the National Association of Indian Youth and a member of the Home Secretary's Race Relations Research Advisory Committee. He has published a number of works in political philosophy.

Professor Alan Little was formerly Director of Reference and Technical Services at the Community Relations Commission. After studying sociology, economics and criminology, he lectured at the London School of Economics between 1959-65. He was Director of Research and Statistics at the Inner London Education Authority between 1967-72. His publications include *Development of Secondary Education,* 1969, and a wide range of articles on race relations, education and criminology in learned journals.

Rt Rev Trevor Huddleston became Bishop of Mauritius in May 1978. He was a priest in South Africa for many years, also serving as Bishop of Masasi between 1960 and 1968. A Vice-President of the Anti-Apartheid Movement and a Trustee of the Runnymede Trust, his publications include *Naught for Your Comfort,* 1956; *The True and Living God,* 1964 and *God's World,* 1966.

Race in the Inner City
John Rex, Professor of Sociology,
University of Warwick

Not long after the Notting Hill riots of 1958, I took part in a meeting organized there by the New Left, to discuss what was to be done. We decided to conduct a survey of housing conditions, because it was unanimously agreed that the real problem was not race, but rotten and decaying housing. Ten years later, when Richard Nixon unveiled his running mate for the Presidential elections after the revolt in the ghettoes, he introduced Spiro Agnew as someone who knew about the problems of the cities. Thus, from Left to Right across the political spectrum, there was a consensus to the effect that if you dealt with the inner-city you would go far towards solving race relations problems. In England, when the question of immigration dominated the election of 1964, Harold Wilson argued that the real problem was one of deficient social services and that an attack on disadvantage would effectively put an end to racism. Dark forebodings that we too would have an American future in race relations if we didn't take action, led eventually to the notion that there were areas of multiple deprivation in the inner-city and that Inner-City Policy must be a focus of major government concern.

Those who have actually studied the Government's White Paper on Inner-City Policy published in 1977 will know that it does not actually claim to have any implications for race relations at all. It says specifically that the problem of race relations is a matter for the Commission for Racial Equality rather than for the Department of the Environment and, far from offering systematic aid to the present residents of the inner-city, it suggests that many of the unskilled, the semi-skilled and the retired who live there may have to move on if the inner-city prospers. Nonetheless it seems clear that there is a widespread belief that inner-city policy is race relations policy, and the Minister of the Environment has gone on record as suggesting that the White Paper is an important contribution to the fight against racism.

For the past fifteen years I have worked with colleagues studying race in the inner-city of Birmingham, first in Sparkbrook in the early sixties and then more recently in the four wards known collectively as Handsworth. Since Sparkbrook is immediately across the tracks from Small Heath, one of the three areas which were studied in formulating the Inner-City Policy and, in any case, both areas have much in common with Small Heath, we are particularly well placed, I think, to assess whether bad race relations are the product of inner-city deprivation and whether better race relations are likely to occur from inner-city improvement. I propose to discuss this by considering, first, what the inner-city looks like and what can be done to make it aesthetically and socially a more satisfying place, and then to ask whether the real cause of anxiety and concern is not race. In fact, I will suggest, that so far from being caused by environmental deterioration, the perception of that deterioration is more bitter because it has racial overtones, and that any attempt to deal with environmental matters only will leave the root cause of anxiety untouched.

In the immediate post-war years, the city of Birmingham scheduled some 50,000 small working class cottages as slums due for demolition. Today that process is nearly complete. Yet is is clear that, quite apart from any question of race, an environmental problem remains. The expectation built into the planning policies of 1945 was that in the foreseeable future the city would be a better place to live in. But now that slum clearance has run its course, there seems to be universal agreement that the total environment where the slums once stood is more depressing than ever.

For the past ten years the slum clearance areas have looked like bomb sites. The buildings and places which survive do so on islands in a sea of rubble and ash. When the slums were there they supported an organic community life and each building, each activity, fitted in as part of the whole. But now that they have been destroyed, nothing meaningful appears to remain, or, rather those activities which do go on do not seem to have any meaningful relation to the place. They happen there because it is an empty stage which no-one is using any more.

Typical of the inner-city in this sense is the Birmingham City Football Ground. Standing in unsplendid isolation on what is now wasteland on the edge of Small Heath, it brings into the area a stage army on twenty or so Saturdays a year who come and cheer and then go away again with little concern any more for the place where they have done their cheering. Even they, however, have revolted recently. 'The ground' says the leader of the revolt, 'is a slum', thus putting his finger on the fact that the demolition of houses creates rather than solves problems of the inner-city.

Of course, the very existence of League Football grounds marks the spot where vibrant working class communities once flourished. But they have now gone and have left only traces. Equally there are traces of a grander life style which has also now disappeared. Quite surprisingly, nearly every inner-city area in Birmingham has a splendid park. Usually there is a lake, rolling green hills and fields, fine trees and in the middle somewhere, a bandstand. And alongside these amenities there are fine terraces and villas where the middle classes once lived. But the parks are now empty of people, waste paper blows against the bandstand, which is rotting away, and the old villas have been turned into rooming houses.

If the poorer working classes have moved to suburban council estates and the medium middle classes to Solihull and Sutton Coldfield, there are some who remain, and there are houses which still perform the same function which they have always performed of housing individual families. These are the medium size terrace houses which have now been saved from any further demolition programme and have been grouped together into general improvement and housing action areas. There are some people in these houses, mainly old people, who have always lived there and it is they, above all, who resist the notion that these areas should be bulldozed away. But their children have left and newcomers who can't get anywhere else to live have filled the vacancies. The Council is very busy here, not merely helping people who want to improve their homes, but actually urging others to take the aid that is offered and doing what they can to provide improvements to streets and corners as well as houses. But, for all the jobbing builders' vans that stand around, one gets the sense that it is a losing battle. One day, one supposes, the Council will give up. These too will be recognised as slums and the demolition process will continue.

A new element has now come upon the scene in the inner-city in the form of the tower block. Somehow it doesn't seem to be what Le Corbusier and the planners who wrote those post-war Pelicans intended. The public spaces either haven't yet been developed or are more meanly conceived, and the corridors and lifts are places of horror. In fact these places were always suspect. They had no legitimacy in the minds of the public as suburban family housing had, and those who were placed there felt that they had been cheated. Along with the decaying elements, therefore, that which had been conceived as part of the brave new world was part of the problem.

Finally, of course, in the large city, each inner-city ward always had its High Street which represented the focal point at which all the strands of community life came together. It remains now only as a ghostly shell. Some of its shops are boarded up, others have been taken over by Indian drapers and grocers who meet the special needs of their own communities more than they do those of the community as a whole. Such new shops as there are, are located in the little precincts around the tower blocks and serve only the people who live there. The people who live in this area are not bound together by this commerce. The style and location of the shops merely serves to underline the fact that the community has come apart.

The Department of the Environment is proposing to bring unused land into use, to make industrial as well as residential improvement areas, to encourage industry to come back or to start up on the disused sites. At the same time the councils are to be encouraged to intensify the street-by-street action to improve and save the remaining terraces. But will that really deal with the problems which are worrying the people of the area? Will it really make Small Heath, Handsworth, Sparkbrook, the sort of places that people want them to be? I think not, and I want to talk to you about the kind of problem which Robert Moore and I found in Sparkbrook in the '60s, and which my colleagues and I at the University of Warwick have been finding in Handsworth during the past four years.

Sparkbrook became known as a problem before the word 'inner-city' was the favoured term to describe urban pathology. The favoured term at that time was 'twilight zone', and Robert Moore and I set out in 1963 to analyse and describe its sociology. Sparkbrook, we discovered, was divided, like Gaul, into three parts. Firstly, there were the scheduled slums — and you knew these were scheduled slums because the very thoughtful Council had pasted little paper notices on the walls outside to say that they were. Secondly, there were the preservable and slightly better houses occupied by single families. But thirdly, there were the biggest houses of all, in which paradoxically, the worst housing conditions of all were to be found. While we were doing our work in Sparkbrook, the Milner Holland Committee commenting on the state of affairs in London noted this fact — that the worst housing in London was no longer in the poor working class East End, but in the West End, in places like Notting Hill. We quickly came to see that the available political and social theories didn't explain the facts of the Sparkbrook situation, and we had to put our own — let me confess it — left-wing, socialist prejudices to one side and try to come up with explanations which actually worked.

It seemed to us that the housing system of Birmigham as a whole was not working. Rather, it was working for, because it was run by, privileged and powerful groups. A lot of people will assent to that and then not expect me to say the next thing that I'm going to say. It was run by privileged and powerful groups, the middle classes on the one hand, who had enough money and property to look after themselves, and the established workers on the other hand who had the Labour Party, through which they could act collectively administering housing resources on their own behalf. The building societies, on the one hand, and the City Council Housing Department on the other, therefore, were in the business of deciding who should have such scarce resources as were available. On the whole they made no provision for problem people and they made no provision for immigrants. If these people were not to sleep on the tracks and in the parks, a secondary housing system — a net beneath the net of the welfare state — has to be created. In the case of housing, that secondary system was provided by the immigrant landlord.

It's of some interest to note that towards the end of the fifties some Tory Ministers — and I'm not sure that Enoch Powell was not one of them — argued against continuing rent controls, suggesting that supply and demand in housing by the late fifties could be brought into balance if the protected tenants of some of the big inner city houses moved on and made way for a more intensive use of those houses. This is actually what happened. Some immigrants — in Sparkbrook they were mostly Pakistanis — concerned to establish a base for their families whom they hoped would follow them and unable to obtain any housing finance through normal channels, found that they could embark on the expensive operation of buying one of the large houses in the area with the aid of a five-year bank loan, if they took in tenants from other groups to occupy their spare rooms at exorbitant rents.

The typical lodging house involved an owner and a few of his fellow villagers or kinsmen who paid virtually no rent, and four or five other domestic units including either immigrant families from other immigrant groups, or English people who for one reason or another could not get housing anywhere else. Irish and West Indian families then, groups of nomadic Irish tinkers, mothers with illegitimate babies, the homeless, discharged prisoners and mental patients, drug addicts and prostitutes — anyone who had no place to go — could find a home here. The interesting point in the film *Cathy Come Home* which is hardly ever noticed, is that when Cathy was really in trouble about housing, she said *'when you're in trouble and you want housing, immigrant landlords are the best, because immigrant landlords ask no questions and they gave you a roof over your head'*. Even Rachmann, the prince amongst lodging house proprietors, is said to have told a leading councillor in the London County Council that the Labour Party should call off their attack on him because he was doing something which the G.L.C. was not in fact doing, namely putting roofs over people's heads. There was a certain point in that.

The lodging house zone, which was created in this way, was not, let me emphasise a ghetto. How could it be? Because the proprietors, in performing what was a charitable service for their own friends and fellow countrymen, had to make money out of people who were not their own friends and fellow countrymen. They had to be drawn from other groups whom it was permissible to extract money from, so the lodging house was necessarily multi-racial. This led some sociologists — of the kind who look only at figures and have a kind of educated incompetence — to the rather absurd conclusion that race relations could not be all that bad because the actual index of segregation was low. What they did not see was that the nature of the multi-racial contact which was going on was such that it exacerbated race relations far more than total ghettoization would have done. The tenants of the scheduled slums — the little red brick houses awaiting demolition, across the High Street, produced a false, but entirely understandable, diagnosis of their situation. It went something like this: 'We've been living in these slums for years waiting rehousing. We couldn't afford to buy big houses and wouldn't even have tried to buy those big old houses across the road. But while we've been waiting to be rehoused these coloured immigrants have come in and bought what are the best houses in the neighbourhood and turned them into slums.' The immigrants, according to this diagnosis, were not only privileged in the housing market. They were also irresponsible and they were making the total housing situation worse. People who believed these things responded when right-wing groups put leaflets through their letter boxes saying 'House Britons, not Blacks'.

Now let me make my position entirely clear here. I want to emphasize that the diagnosis which I have just given you, understandable though it is, is entirely and utterly false. The immigrants, landlord and tenant alike, were as much victims of the situation as they were its cause. But someone had to be blamed in a situation in which people were looking for someone to blame, and the Public Health Department seemed to be making it clear, with its crusade against the lodging houses, where they thought the blame to lie. Nearly every week, while we were working in Sparkbrook, another batch of landlords were brought before the courts and nearly all of them were Asians. All public definitions of the situation seem therefore to confirm the diagnosis of the slum tenant.

The Public Health Department could hardly be blamed for what it did, either. Its inspectors, after all, were not concerned with the diagnosis of long-term causes and with the overall determination of social policy. They had to eliminate a particular evil — multiple occupation — and the way to do it for them seemed to be to stop the man who was the immediate perpetrator of that evil. I used to love one particular Public Health Inspector in Birmingham. He used to stand on the street corner cleaning his finger nails and looking like a character out of Graham Greene waiting to pounce. But the real dilemma which faced the Public Health Inspectors was that they weren't allowed to put the lodging house proprietors out of business, because the City was implicitly relying upon these people to do the work it was failing to do. All that could be done, therefore, was to let the landlord do the job which he was doing — this pariah landlord, this easily blamable landlord — and when he had done the job to punish him for it. It's difficult to imagine a nastier outcome of the race relations situation. People sometimes say immigrants are a scapegoat, but that suggests just some kind of psychological fantasy. What I am saying here is that immigrants had been in a sense, set up so that they were in a situation in which it was possible to blame them.

Well now, Sparkbrook, was not — as we later found — the real typical inner city phenomenon. It represented one phase of the inner city's development which was particularly important as single men flooded in to beat the ban on immigration which was imposed in 1962. It still exists and it still has that lodging house complex. The more typical phenomenon is that which exists in the four wards which are collectively known as Handsworth. They nestle down just below Spaghetti Junction between the Aston Villa and the West Bromwich football grounds. This is the new 'Inner-City', but as I shall show, its problems are not simply inner city problems, they too have a markedly racial dimension. Handsworth has become a cauldron of racial conflict because discriminatory policies have forced people to live in juxtaposition with each other in an unhappy state of racial conflict.

Immigrants from the West Indies and Asia, who came during the 1950s and '60s, were not likely to be satisfied for long with the accommodation which was offered in the lodging houses. They found much better long-term solutions for their probems through house purchase for single family occupation. And there was one avenue opened up to them by the official housing policy of the city.

Given that privately rented accommodation was fast disappearing from the scene, and given that the local authority was reluctant to let them rent in the public sector, immigrants were forced to buy houses. There's a common notion amongst sociologists of housing and urban sociologists that the people who are least well off in the housing system are those who are forced to rent. This is a point which has been made by my colleague Ray Parr at Kent. The point that I want to make is that less fortunate than those who are forced to rent are some who are forced to buy. These are people who could not afford, or faced discrimination from estate agents and vendors in trying to buy into, semi-detached suburbia; but they found that, while the Building Societies would not lend on inner-city property, the local authority were quite willing to, and indeed positively offered, as an alternative, to let immigrants have mortgages on houses in the inner city. So that an immigrant found that it was very very difficult indeed — you had to wait five years to go on the list — and then, when you did get on the list, you went into a very poor house, so it was very difficult to get into council housing. But there was this way forward: you could get a mortgage from the city council — the City Council was actually very helpful — and while the building societies, as they say, 'red-lined' the area and said 'that's not an area where we would lend', the local authority said 'these are precisely the areas in which we would like you to go — in which we will give you mortgages.' Moreover, the increasingly important Housing Associations also found that they could borrow money for converting terrace houses into flats. They were encouraged to use alternative criteria, without any element of discrimination against immigrants, in selecting tenants — alternative criteria to those used by the Council.

Amongst the people whom we've interviewed, we found that in the West Indian community, as many people got their houses by the rather unusual method of getting a local authority mortgage or of renting a house or a flat from a Housing Association, as did through Building Societies — about equal percentages went to Building Societies or got a local authority mortgage or went into a Housing Association conversion. Asians also used local authority mortgages, but they still resorted, as we found them resorting before, to short-term bank loans.

In this way, through the business of local authority mortgages in the improvement areas, the local authority solved its problems of housing the bulk of immigrants with families, and this was the way, in the '60s, of housing the immigrants. It took a lot of them off the council housing list. The immigrants, too, solved their problem, by getting a whole house for the family to grow up in and one which they found they could actually get financial aid to improve. In this way one soon had in Handsworth in Birmingham a population of property-owning West Indian and Asian burghers who had settled down in their jobs and worked out a pattern of community life in what was for them a home from home. We found that the Asian and West Indian householders of Handsworth were an extraordinarily stable population. They had mainly been there ten to twenty years and most of them had been in their existing employment for five years — a very solid section of the working class. Unfortunately, there was one group for whom the presence of these people created a very severe problem indeed. This was the group of British born, Birmingham born, ward-born Englishmen who had remained and who hadn't taken flight. There's one ward in Birmingham, the one which has the heaviest immigrant population — the Soho ward — which can, I think, serve as an example of the kind of transformation which has occurred. In 1951 there were very few foreigners there. In 1961 this area had 10½% of its population born in the West Indies and just under 3% Asian. In 1971 nearly 30% of the population were born in the New Commonwealth and the majority of these — 18½% — were Asian. The West Indians were superseded by the Asians but there were not two communities together and, of course, they had begun to have children. The statistics for 1971 for that ward for people with both parents born in the New Commonwealth — that obviously includes the children — showed that 49% of the population of that ward in 1971 were in fact immigrants or the descendants of immigrants. With the immigrants being concentrated in the child-bearing age groups, it seems certain to me that the whites in that particular ward are now in a minority and the West Indians are now outnumbered by the later coming Asians.

It's also obvious from the age structure of the white population that many young people have fled. In our sample of respondents, 50% of the white people were over 60. They were, or had been, mostly in skilled or white-collar work and had always lived in this area close to jobs in the City Centre. They could remember Handsworth Park in its days of glory and, since this was their home, they were disinclined to leave, even if, as occasionally happened in the Housing Action Areas, the Council suggested that their houses should be demolished.

What these people wanted — and I have a great deal of feeling for them — they are not stupid racists who lived there — what many of them feel is that they wanted this as their place where they could retire in peace and quiet. And for such people — people with strictly conservative, with a small 'c', views of the world and who'd been brought up in the city of Joseph Chamberlain, a city of imperialism — what happened was nothing less than a disaster. The Soho Road, for them, suddenly came to look like a street in Bombay, and little knots of West Indian boys stood around on the streets wearing strange Rasta locks and little Rasta hats, and sometimes these boys would get into trouble with the police. These Englishmen, who'd grown up in Birmingham and had learned to think of the peoples of the Empire as their inferiors, now found that they were supposed to live as neighbours. They felt threatened and de-statussed. The one thing that they said repeatedly was, 'We weren't asked'. And that's quite true. They weren't. What happened was that policy decisions were taken with a view to keeping the immigrants out elsewhere and they were literally funnelled into places like Handsworth. In other words, in order to avoid facing up to race relations problems, particularly in the suburbs, the local authorities were developing a policy of de-facto segregation. But it was worse than that — they were funnelling the immigrants in to live amongst people who were bound not to want them living there.

The authorities avoided the accusation that they were producing bad race relations through segregation by saying in their best liberal tones that the problem wasn't a problem of race but one of housing. It set about its task of getting housing improvement going with great urgency. The local whites, however, read it differently. They accepted that the housing was deteriorating, but they put it down to the presence of blacks, and no amount of environmental improvement was likely to change their conviction. Indeed, there is much evidence to show that immigrant home-owners were actually improving the area physically. But if the real deterioration — in the minds of these people, their white neighbours — consisted of having blacks there at all, then no amount of physical alteration of environment was going to change that.

The problems which existed in the sphere of housing were multiplied in the schools. Because there was such a high degree of immigrant concentration, and because immigrant fertility was higher than whites', quite obviously the schools would be more overwhelmingly black than the neighbourhoods'. Secondary schools with more than 60% of their children from immigrant homes were the norm in that part of Birmingham, and in some primary schools would be more overwhelmingly black than the neighbourhoods' cultural and educational transactions which go on between teachers and immigrant children on the one hand, and teachers and white British children on the other, these schools presented something of a problem. They presented a problem for the immigrant children in that separate education was no more likely to be equal in Birmingham, England, than it was in Birmingham, Alabama, and a problem for the white child too, who found himself in a school which had perforce to deal most of the time with the special problems of immigrants.

The New Inner City was not Sparkbrook. It was a place now where young hardworking and thrifty immigrants had found themselves a community base, making the most of their housing and jobs and enjoying the security and protection of a close-knit ethnic community. On the whole, they spoke well of the area and their jobs, even of the schools. But there was a total asymmetry between the attitudes disclosed by blacks and those disclosed by whites. The West Indians, and even more the Asians, were inclined to believe that the races got on perfectly well together, whereas the overwhelming majority of the whites believed that race relations were bad. Despite programmes of environmental improvement and despite the burgherly stability of the now settled immigrant generation, the area now was one apparently destined for continuing and possibly escalating racial conflict.

The Asians in this situation were most likely to turn the other cheek — or to put it another way, with their eyes firmly on the economic opportunities which are open to them, they didn't notice what was hitting them. They lived in spartan conditions, saved money, and organised themselves through kin-based organisations to help their children to educational and economic advancement. In the meantime they appear not to want to be incorporated into the society. Indeed, maintaining their separateness is a way of maintaining their communal strength and mobilising resources to help the next generation to success. The West Indians, speaking English and having English working-class aspirations for themselves and their children, were much more frustrated by discrimination and failure. Black unemployment amongst the young is high. Our estimate is that nearly half of the 15 to 25 year old age group among Jamaicans accept the Rastafarian diagnosis of their situation as one of living in Babylon. It's said that there was a point in the development of the black revolution — or the revolt of the ghettos in the United States — when Stokely Carmichael literally breathed into a microphone the words 'Black Power'. The word Babylon now has a meaning which is immediately understood by every young West Indian. And for most, it is a summation of the situation — something which explains to a man the kind of captivity in which he lives and which gives to him a sense of his own identity. Ultimately it is true that a lot of this talk may be expressive, rather than revolutionary. The cult of Black Power may be merely a means of guaranteeing to an individual the security and identity which he needs to succeed in a competitive world. For the moment, however, one can't see bridges being built between black and white. Those that do exist appear, to young West Indians at least, to have been torn up by whites and, despite what I call the burgherly conservatism of the immigrant generation, nearly all immigrants are inclined to rely upon self-help or the help of kin, rather than upon goodwill and the paternalism of the whites, even though the whites become more and more energetic on that front.

What then should be done about this situation? The answer which has been coming to me from those closer to government than I am goes something like this — and I've almost literally had this message — 'Tell us how we can spend money in ways which will help immigrants and promote integration without our having to say what we are doing. Just let it be a financial transaction. Tell us where we can spend money but don't ask us to have a positive race relations policy.' I need hardly say that when I'm asked for this sort of advice by people in Government I refuse to answer the question. Money, it seems to me, is hardly the issue. Yes — we could have more, but government is spending some, and more interestingly, the immigrants are building up their own resources. But what really has to be unknotted is the tangle of social relations which has forced immigrants into institutionalised situations of conflicts with Englishmen over housing, and that requires not a low profile race relations policy, but a serious non-party high profile policy.

Let me then make my position very, very clear. I am arguing that fear produces discrimination and it is discrimination which forces immigrant minorities into situations of conflict in the inner city. These situations are not due simply to environmental problems. They arise, primarily, because native-born residents are forced into competition with people whose behaviour they fear and whose cultures they do not understand. What has to be done, therefore, is to end the discrimination which forces the immigrants into this intense and fearful competition and conflict, and to promote knowledge and understanding of their culture and social organization among the whites.

Before I detail the things I think need to be done, let me just recall the idological horror which has occurred in East London since I wrote this. The Bengalis are said to have asked for a ghetto because they are afraid of the attacks which have been made on their members when they live in more dispersed conditions. Granting them that ghetto is no answer to the problem. This is where we need a high profile race relations policy so that Bengalis and others will be able to go about their lawful occasions in peace and fully protected.

The first thing which would have to be done, it seems to me, in order to arrest the escalation of conflict between the races, is for all the political parties at the highest level to commit themselves to a positive race relations policy. I think it is unlikely but I don't think it is impossible. I would like to see Merlyn Rees, William Whitelaw and David Steele join together in a non-party political broadcast, in which they would make it clear that they had nothing to offer the racists, that the debate about immigration numbers was over, and that they were all determined that West Indian and Asian descended people in Britain would have the same rights as any other citizen. If this isn't done, if one party believes that it can gain electoral advantage by being more anti-black than the others, there can't possibly be even a beginning to the process of producing neighbourly relations between black and white. It would be nice to leave that element out of the situation, to suggest that we could ignore the politicans and get on with the job. But in my view, without that political affirmation, the idea that we can do something when we, through our political representatives, are bidding for the racist vote, seems to me to be a delusion.

Secondly, there must be a sustained civil rights policy, and so far as the inner city is concerned, this means that any policy of forced concentration or of forced dispersal must be outlawed. Legal sanctions will be important in achieving this, but far more can be done as well by other means over and above the legal minimum. We need well-organized and independent and militant minority organisations who will press the minority case in all areas for better jobs, for better homes, for better schools. One of the sad and simple facts about Britain today is that there is no British organisation amongst the immigrants as effective as the National Association for the Advancement of the Coloured People was in the United States, even though that organisation has long since been by-passed by others, which are far more militant and effective. The minorities in England need, and Britain needs, the most effective immigrant and minority organisations possible.

The third policy development which is necessary is a programme of multi-cultural education, both of adults, through the media, and of children, through the school. By this I do not mean a programme for educating immigrants or a programme for those who live in immigrant areas. What is most important in Britain today is that all people and particularly people in all-white areas and those who occupy prestigious and powerful positions, should achieve a better and more sympathetic understanding of the minorities who live amongst us.

This point is very rarely understood. Most people who think about multi-cultural education at all, think of teaching immigrants British ways, on the one hand, and taking a patronising interest in immigrant customs on the other. What I am suggesting is that we learn about the history, the culture and the social organisation of, say, the Sikhs, and the part they've played in the Empire, and come to see them as different from ourselves in the way the French are, but **not** as inferior. If you really get to know Sikhs you will find that the thought has never occurred to them. Now the same is true of all the other ethnicities and it's true also of the self-assertive cultures of resistance which one finds — most especially the dominant one amongst West Indian youth, that of Rastafari. All of these are ways in which people attain dignity and self-respect in the way of degrading discrimination, even though at the same time by being alien, by being apparently aggressive, they may serve to escalate racial tension. It's necessary that we should begin to understand these cultures, and speaking as an amateur anthropologist, the closer I get to studying the ethnicity of the immigrants, the closer I get to studying the cultures of resistance and of affirmation which exist amongst them, the more impressed I am by their seriousness, by the way in which they help to give people dignity. They are serious cultures amongst people who are our neighbours and who have every reason to deserve our respect.

But finally, it's no use our giving people cultural recognition if we don't give them the means of industrial and political representation. A great deal here depends on the industrial and political labour movement. There have been a number of industrial disputes in which the big unions have neglected the interests of their immigrant members. In those cases, the immigrants have forced them eventually to appoint minority shop-stewards. These shop-stewards have then played their part in deracialising trade unionism.

A similar process of deracialisation has to be accomplished in politics. It is true, of course, that the political parties stand to lose votes by appearing anti-racist. But it is also becoming true that in inner-city wards they can't win without immigrant support. Let them therefore adopt immigrant candidates and see whether by making the immigrants cause their own, they can't build up their own strength. Why should a place like Handsworth — or the Soho ward with the sort of population which it has — not be represented by someone of West Indian or Indian descent? Why is it that our political system has not found ways of allowing for official articulation of the views of these people? Why do we deal with their problems simply through the techniques of paternalism, appointing our chosen people to represent these immigrant communities? One sometimes feels that, at worst, the paternalistic system which we've evolved for dealing with minority problems is similar to that in South Africa where you have a Ministry of Education, a Ministry of Health and so on, but all affairs of the black people and taken care of by the Bantu Affairs Department. Don't we sometimes think about immigrants in this way? Don't we in fact see the whole question of how their rights are being — are to be dealt with, as one of paternalism? Could we not envisage the development of a British political system in which immigrants speak for themselves? I think there are some signs of a breakthrough in this direction but we have a long way to go.

A high profile race relations programme of the sort which I am suggesting would make the co-existence of culturally distinct communities possible. Indeed, if it were successfully carried through, possibly people might actually come to take delight in the diversity of British society. When I went to Canada, I was astonished to realise how Canada was changed. With the number of Chinese, Black, Latino faces one saw in the street, the very notion of Canadian identity one felt was something which had not yet been forged. The immigration of people from the poorer countries to the richer countries in North West Europe is producing new nations in the same way. Part of the British nation is going to consist of Indian-descended and West Indian-descended people. Surely it is possible that one day, knowing that we might regard our Britishness as enhanced by this, we might come to take delight in the diversity of British society. Of course, some children in the minorities will lose their culture and pass into the mainstream. Indeed, if language and accent were all, one might say that this had already happened. But the more fundamental problem is that of the co-existence of culturally distinct communities and that problem remains.

How far does all this bear on the inner-city? A great deal, I think, for if the sort of cultural and political situation which I have suggested were achieved, much of the inner city anxiety which exists at the moment would disappear. On the other hand, if *in addition* to a serious race relations policy we carried through an environmental and economic improvement, in which the minorities also participated, the effect would be even greater. **What is not possible, however,** and this is the message of my paper, **is that racial conflict will somehow go away just because the inner city has been made beautiful.** Unfortunately, it's just this belief which informs most of our social policy thinking at the moment.

Now in this talk, I've described a situation in which my likely prognosis is that nothing effective will be done in the sphere of race relations policy. And sometimes, when I'm doing sociology, I say it's not my task to provide a happy ending. I, as a sociologist, should simply describe what I see. But what I've been seeking to do in the end of my paper, is to talk about what seemed to me the essential pre-conditions of stopping the escalation of racial conflict in the inner city. I don't believe that it is very likely that what I'm asking for will happen — especially given the lack of political will. But to accept this fatalistically is to opt out of responsibility and I do believe that unless these steps are taken, we won't avoid a continuation and escalation of the conflict.

Racism and Reaction — Dr Stuart Hall
Director of the Centre for Cultural Studies,
University of Birmingham

In his book *Black and White*[1] which is a study of the negro in English society 1555 to 1945 by James Walvin — a book worth reading — he recounts how in the last decade of the 16th Century, England was troubled by an expanding population and a shortage of food. He said *as hunger swept the land, England was faced by a problem which taxed the resources of government to the limits.* He adds that *immigrants added to the problem,* since *no group was so immediately visible as the blacks* — which, it may surprise you to know, by then had been distributed already in their thousands in English cities as a result of the growing involvement of England in the slave trade. Queen Elizabeth I accordingly wrote to the Lord Mayors of the country's major cities and remarked that *there are of late divers blackamores brought into the realm, of which kind of people there are alreadie here to manie, consideryng howe God hath blessed this land with a great increase of people.* And she recommended *that those kind of people be sent forth of the land.* And indeed, in January 1601, she repeated her advice in a rather more official form of a Royal Proclamation allowing a Lübeck merchant to take *such Negroes and blackamores which are carried into this realm, to the great annoyance of her own liege people.*

Walvin doesn't record whether this is the first British 'moral panic' about race. But the incident does give us a little bit of historical perspective on the theme of this lecture, which is about the English reaction to race in the post-war period. It also suggests something about the mechanism involved: that it isn't quite of such recent origin as we might suppose. I mean, specifically, the mechanism by which problems which are internal to British society, not ones which are visited on it from the outside, come to be projected on to, or exported into, an excessive preoccupation with the problem of 'race'. This decade is not the first time that the English official mind, when forced to contemplate a 'crisis', has turned the conversation in the direction of 'the blacks'.

This is, in a way, the first and perhaps the most important point that I want to make. Let me put it rather more generally. There is, it seems to me, an overwhelming tendency to abstract questions of race from what one might call their *internal* social and political basis and contexts in British society — that is to say, to deal with 'race' as if it has nothing intrinsically to do with the present 'condition of England'. It's viewed rather as an 'external' problem, which has been foisted to some extent on English society from the outside: it's been visited on us, as it were, from the skies. To hear problems of race discussed in England today, you would sometimes believe that relations between British people and the peoples of the Caribbean or the Indian sub-continent began with the wave of black immigrants in the late forties and fifties. 'The English and race' is frequently debated as if it is a brief and indeed temporary interlude, which will shortly be brought to an end. These poor, benighted people, for reasons which the British sometimes find it hard to bring to mind, picked themselves up out of their villages and plantations and, quite uninvited, made this long, strange and apparently unpredictable journey to the doors of British industry — which, as you know, out of the goodness of their hearts, gave them jobs. Now the 'good times' are over, the kissing has to stop. The national patience is exhausted. The fund of goodwill has been used up. It's time the problem 'went back where it came from'. The British people, I am told, require to be assured that the problem of race will have a definite and conclusive end.

It seems to me that the tendency to pull race out from the internal dynamic of British society, and to repress its history, is not, as might be supposed, confined to the political 'Right' of the spectrum. It is also, in my opinion, to be found on the liberal 'Left'. For the 'Right', immigration and race has become a problem of the control of an external flow, or as the popular press is fond of saying, 'a tidal wave': cut off the flow and racism will subside. The liberal 'Left', on the other hand, have long treated race and immigration as a problem in the exercise of 'good conscience': Be kind to 'our friends from overseas': then racism will disappear. Neither side can nowadays bring themselves to refer to Britain's imperial and colonial past, even as a contributory factor to the present situation. The slate has been wiped clean. Racism is not endemic to the British social formation. It has nothing intrinsically to do with the dynamic of British politics, or with the economic crisis. It is not part of the English culture, which now has to be indeed protected against pollution — it does not belong to the 'English ideology'. It's an external virus somehow injected into the body politic and it's matter of **policy** whether we can deal with it or not — it's not a matter of **politics**.

I hope to persuade you that this view cannot be true. It is not true of the historical past. And it is certainly not true of the decades since the 1950s, the 'high tide' of post-war black migration to Britain. We can't account for the emergence of a specifically **indigenous** British racism in this way. This last phase, the 50s, 60s and 70s, is of course the main subject I want to come on to in a moment. But something first must be said about the historical aspects. Britain's relations with the peoples of the Caribbean and the Indian sub-continent do not, of course, belong to and begin in the 1940s. British attitudes to the ex-colonial subject peoples of a former time cannot be accurately charted from the appearance of a black proletariat in Birmingham or Bradford in the 1950s. These relations have been central features in the formation of Britain's material prosperity and dominance, as they are now central themes in English culture and in popular and official ideologies. That story should not indeed require to be rehearsed. Britain's rise to mercantile dominance and the process of generating the surpluses of wealth which set economic development in motion, were founded on the slave trade and the plantation system in the Americas in the Seventeenth Century. India provided the basis for the foundation of Britain's Asian Empire in the Eighteenth; the penetration by trade of Latin America and of the Far East was the centre-piece of Britain's industrial and imperial hegemony in the Nineteenth. In each of these phases, an economic and cultural chain — in short, to be brutal, the imperialist chain — has bound the fate of millions of workers and peasants in the colonial hinterlands to the destiny of rich and poor in the heartland of English society. The wealth — drawn off through conquest, colonization and trade — has slightly enriched one English class after another. It has supported the foundation of one flourishing urban culture after another. It has led to one phase of economic development after another. It is, in a sense, geography and distance which has rendered this long historical connection invisible. It's only in the very last phase of British imperialism that the labouring classes of the satellite countries and the labouring classes of the metropolis have had to confront one another directly 'on native ground' in large numbers. But that is not the same thing as saying that their fates have not long been indissolubly connected.

I want to make the proposition that the very definition in the 1970s of what it is to be English, has been articulated around this. If the blood of the colonial workers has not mingled extensively with the English, then their labour-power has long entered the economic blood-stream of British society. It is in the sugar you stir; it is in the sinews of the famous British 'sweet tooth'; it is in the tea-leaves at the bottom of the next 'British' cuppa.

I want to turn on that point and argue that the development of an indigenous British racism in the post-war period **begins** with the profound historical forgetfulness — what I want to call the loss of historical memory, a kind of historical amnesia, a decisive mental repression — which has overtaken the British people about race and Empire since the 1950s. Paradoxically, it seems to me, the native, home-grown variety of racism begins with this attempt to wipe out and efface every trace of the colonial and imperial past. Clearly, that is one effect of the traumatic adjustment to the very process of bringing Empire to an end. But, undoubtedly, it has left an enormous reservoir of guilt and a deep, historical, resentment. It's not possible to operate surgically so directly on popular memory without leaving scars and traces. And, undoubtedly, this reservoir of resentment and guilt, which does not find easy expression any longer in, for instance, the forms of popular imperialism in which it did at the end of the 19th Century, but which is nevertheless there, has undoubtedly nourished and provides something of a reservoir for the indigenous racism of the 50s and 60s. Its lingering legacy may in fact account for something of racism's popular appeal in the last twenty years. Thus, that history has to be reckoned with, by one way or another. But it cannot alone explain the growth of a home-grown racism in Britain in the last 20 years.

To do this, we have to turn to the factors which are more internal to British society, factors which have made racism a growing and dynamic political force in Britain since the 1950s. And here perhaps I should say that it's not helpful to define racism as a 'natural' and permanent feature — either of all societies or indeed of a sort of universal 'human nature'. It's not a permanent human or social deposit which is simply waiting there to be triggered off when the circumstances are right. It has no natural and universal law of development. It does not always assume the same shape. There have been many signficantly different **racisms** — each historically specific and articulated in a different way with the societies in which they appear. Racism is always historically specific in this way, whatever common features it may appear to share with other similar social phenomena. Though it may draw on the cultural and ideo- logical traces which are deposited in a society by previous historical phases, it always assumes specific forms which arise out of **present** — not the past — conditions and organisation of society. It may matter less that Britain has, over four centuries, been involved in modes of economic exploitation and political dominance, on a world scale, which frequently operated through the mechanism of race. This only signals the potential — perhaps, the propensity — of the society to travel that route again. But the indigenous racism of the 60s and 70s is significantly different, in form and effect, from the racism of the 'high' colonial period. It is a racism 'at home', not abroad; it is the racism, not of a dominant but of a declining social formation. It is to the construction of this home grown variety that I want now to turn.

First, it's necessary to establish some kind of rough periodization. But in doing this, I ask you to hold two different perspectives in mind at the same time. I think we must look, what I call **sequentially,** at the way in which racism has been constructed and developed through the three decades; at its development as a process; at its forms and its deepening impact from one stage to another. Here we are interested in what the turning points have been. But at the same time, I think it's important to look **laterally** at what are the other things with which this developing racism has been connected.

We start at the period of the late 40s and 50s, the period of initial settlement. Here, we find the build up of black workers in the labour-hungry centres of

British production. It's a period when industry is, of course, swinging over from war-time to peace-time production. It leads in to the great productive 'boom' of the mid 50s. The main outlines of the pattern of black settlement are established in this phase: the inner-city black concentrations, multiple-occupancy, the density of black labour in certain specific occupational sectors. In this period, accommodation and adjustment between blacks and whites is on the agenda. The black population, on the whole, maintain what I would call a 'low profile'. They draw their curtains both against the cold and against the 'outsider'. They efface themselves as an intrusive presence. They are tiptoeing through the tulips. It's a period of muted optimism about the hope and dream of long-term black and white assimilation.

The real environment where this proposition is to be tested is, of course, in the jobs and localities where black and white workers meet and live. There are, indeed, even in this early phase, problems of adjustment between blacks and whites. What is not present are the strictly defined lines of informal segregation between blacks and whites which has come to be the prevailing social pattern in such areas. The whole period is one which Sivanandan has called the 'laissez-faire' period in British immigration politics. It's the period of the 'open door'. Remember that it's lubricated by the economic boom. The need in British industry to draw heavily on this new reserve army of labour weakens both any official resistance to the introduction of a black proletariat and the sense of competition for jobs between blacks and whites. The segmentation of blacks and Asian workers in particular occupational sectors helps in this shielding process. But above all, rising living standards in this period provide just that economic space, just that room for economic manoeuvre, especially in the urban areas, which gives people from different ethnic backgrounds a little room to settle and move in, to put it crudely. The modest 'optimism' about race in this period is closely dependent on a general climate of economic optimism and the one is an expression of the other.

The real history of that early phase remains to be written. But the first signs of an open and emergent racism of a specifically indigenous type appears, of course, in the race riots of Notting Hill and Nottingham in 1958. These riots cannot be directly attributed to the early warning signs of a developing economic crisis, though those are undoubtedly on stage. Notting Hill is a classic scenario for the appearance of indigenous racism: it's one of those 'traditional urban zones' where, for the first time, the incipient 'colony' life of blacks begins for the first time to flourish and expand at the very heart of the British city.

In the race riots of 1958, there are three constituent elements. The first is the appearance, for the first time in real terms since the 1940s, of an active fascist political element: the Unionist movement and the dissident League of Empire Loyalists. They saw, quite correctly, that the uneven development of culture in an area like this, with its incipient but growing urban problems, provided a more favourable terrain for the construction of a native racism than, for example, the more traditional structures of an older area of settlement, like Brixton. They introduced the syntax of racism into street-corner politics for the first time openly in the post-war period. But, in effect, they were at that stage more symptom than cause.

The second element, however, is more important. It is the structured antagonism between 'colony' blacks and sections of the indigenous white working class and petty-bourgeoisie of this decaying 'Royal' suburb. It is against this fulcrum — which marks the interconnection between the politics of race and the politics of the inner city — that the wheel of British racism first begins to turn.

The third, and active element — that which attracted the publicity and the talk — was white teenagers. Here, looking laterally, it is worthwhile reminding you that Notting Hill race riots have two histories, not one. It has a history in the development and the emergence of British racism and also in the panics about youth and affluence and permissiveness in the 1950s. It is part of that double structure. If the presence of blacks within the area touched sources of public anxiety about competition over scarce resources and coming competition over jobs and so on, the spectacle of black and white youths, locked in confrontation around the tube station and the backstreets of North Kensington fed directly into a deep and troubled anxiety about the whole process of post-war social change — a process, incidentally, for which the term 'Youth' had by then become a vivid social metaphor. In its famous editorial *Hooliganism is Hooliganism, The Times* mapped the Notting Hill events directly, not into the problem of race or of urban poverty, but into the problem of hooliganism, teenage violence, lawlessness, anarchy, together with the football spectator — an ancient ring that term has — and the railway carriage breaker — an even more ancient formulation. "All", *The Times* said, "are manifestations of a strand of our social behaviour that an **adult** society can do without". As the economic downturn begins and youth culture surges forward, Britain introduces, in 1962, the first Commonwealth Immigration Act, which imposes controls on the 'flow of black people into the society'.

The second turning point is 1964. For by now, the economic boom has tapered off and the classes which have to be addressed about the growing material problems — which in the 1950s you will remember were defined as never to appear again — are no longer composed of runaway Teddy Boys or football hooligans, but adult white workers, and their families. The location of the new turning point in the emergence of post-war racism, therefore takes place not in the decaying transitional zone of Notting Hill but in the very heartland of traditional and conservative Britain: Smethwick, the Midlands. Peter Griffiths's successful campaign which centred on black immigration in the 1964 election marks the first moment when racism is appropriated into the official policy and programme of a major political party and legitimated as the basis of an electoral appeal, specifically addressed to the popular white classes. Here is the beginning of racism as an element in the official politics of British populism — racism in a structured and 'legitimate' form. The defeat of a Labour Minister on the issues proved the penetration of this ideology into the organised working class and to the labour institutions themselves. It revealed the degree to which, as a consequence, of everything that had happened to the labour movement in the 50s and 60s, sectors of the working class were by now clearly exposed and vulnerable to the construction of a popular racism. The Smethwick victory is a turning point in the history of British racism. It is followed by the 1965 White Paper on Immigration from the Commonwealth, which as Robert Moore has recently observed, *'laid the ideological basis for subsequent policy in this area and as a result, the argument that the numbers of immigrants was the essence of the problem'.*

Between 1964 and 1968, the date of our third 'turning point', it seems that the world itself, not just Smethwick, turned. It turned, of course, specifically about race. The dream of assimilation of black people to white culture is laid low and interned in the mid-60s. The black population draws back into its defensive enclaves and, much affected in the 60s by the rise of black struggles, especially in the United States, begins to develop a different, distinct and more actively engaged political ideology. But 1968 is also, of course, a cataclysmic year, not only in Britain but elsewhere: in the U.S., France, Italy, Germany, Japan and Czechoslovakia. It is the period of growing protests against the Vietnam War. It's the year of the student revolutions, of black power and black separatism, of the cultural underground; of 'hot' summers followed by 'hot' autumns. It inaugurates, in Britain and elsewhere, a period of profound social, cultural and political polarization. It is when the great consensus of the 50s and early 60s comes apart, when the 'politics of the centre' dissolves and reveals the contradictions and social antagonisms which are gathering beneath. It is, more specifically, a period in which the state and the dominant classes perceive, not simply what had tended to transfix them in the 50s, that is to say the plague of 'permissiveness', the loss of traditional standards and landmarks, but something much worse than that — something close to an organised and active conspiracy against the social order itself. It is the year in which President Nixon wins an infamous victory by summoning up the 'silent majority' in the service of 'law and order'.

'Powellism' is formed in this moment, in this crucible. By 'Powellism' I mean something larger and more significant than the enunciation of a specifically defiant policy about race and the black population by a single person. I mean the formation of an 'official' racist policy at the heart of

British political culture. Mr Powell's personal pronouncements on race in 1968 and 1969 have since become justly famous. It is not so frequently remarked that 'Powellism', though it undoubtedly derived its cutting edge from the resonance of its racial themes, was indeed directed more widely at the general crisis of the social order itself; at the conspiracy of radical and alien forces threatening the society, at what Mr Powell himself called the 'Enemy Within'. Nor can the articulation of this talk of 'conspiracy' and 'threats to the social order' be laid exclusively at his door. A range of politicans and public spokesmen in the press and the media in this period are mesmerized by the spectacle of a society which is careering into a social crisis. A crisis of authority.

It is this whole crisis, not race alone, which is the subject and object of the law and order campaigns of the period and the increasingly vigorous appeal to 'tough measures'. But undoubtedly, as far as what one might call the 'crisis' talk in British society is concerned, it is largely thematised through race. Race is the prism through which the British people are called upon to live through, then to understand, and then to deal with the growing crisis. The 'Enemy' is 'within the gates'. 'He' is nameless: 'he' is protean: 'he' is everywhere. He may even, we're told at the one point, be inside the Foreign Office, cooking the immigration figures. But someone will name him. He is 'the Other', he is the stranger in the midst, he is the cuckoo in the nest, he is the excrement in the letterbox. 'He' is — the blacks. This ideology, which is formed in response to a crisis, must of course, to become a real and historical political force, connect with the lived experiences of the 'silent majorities'. It must be given a concrete purchase on the lives of citizens, on their everyday going and comings, on their conditions of existence, if they are to feel that the 'threat to society' is palpable and real. When the 'silent' and beleagured majorities — the great underclasses, the great, silent 'British public' — are made to 'speak' through the ventriloquism of its public articulators, it is not surprising that it 'speaks' with the unmistakeable accent of a thoroughly home-grown racism. In this period 'Powellism' may be kept out of political power. But in this period it dominated and defined the ideological terrain. Both the Act of 1968 with its explicit use of racial categories, and the 1971 Act which succeeded it — bearing down on dependents and families of black and Asian workers —are tributes to its profound and long term success, that is to say, its popular, mobilizing appeal.

It is on the back of that moment that the great backlash of the 70s comes to be constructed. It moves on each of the fronts at once: political, industrial, economic, racial, ideological. As the true depths of the British economic recession begin to be revealed and as the state girds up its loins to confront directly what is called the hidden materialism of the working class, we witness the construction of what I have come to call a 'soft law and order' society. The law itself becomes, in this period, in part the engine of this social regression.

On the industrial front, it is indeed the law which is recruited directly into the confrontation with the working class. On the political front, it is the law which is mobilized against radicals and demonstrators and 'extremists'. It is in this period that the syntax was formed of extremists versus moderates, without which at one stage it seemed impossible for the media to comment on politics at all. The legal harassment of the black colony populations, the overt racist homilies against the whole black population by judges in courts, the imposition of tough policing and arrest on suspicion in the colony areas, the rising hysteria about black crime and the identification of black crime with 'mugging', must all be seen the context of what, in the early 70s, is a decisive turn in the whole society into a form of popular authoritarianism. Here what we had defined earlier as a set of discrete panics about race can no longer be identified in that way. It is impossible to separate them out. The lulls between them now are only temporary: the running warfare between unemployed black youth and the police; the swamping tactics of the Special Patrol Groups in the colony areas; the arrests of black political activists 'on suspicion'; the scare, fanned by sections of the press, against Ugandan and then Malawi Asians — the great, prophesied 'tidal wave' at last. Here are the 'scandalous' stories of Asian families 'living in luxury off the Council' — which is only the black counterpart of that general assault on the welfare state which has produced its white counterpart stories of welfare scroungers drawing their dole on the Costa Brava. There are the beginnings of attacks on black centres and black book shops, the murder of Asian youths, the confrontations in Brockwell Park and other scenes of set warfare, the fining and focussing down of the problem of race into its concrete conditions in the inner-city. In these areas, the programmes of urban aid have failed to stem the tide of poverty and decay. The cycles of unemployment and the fears of recession are beginning to bite. Young blacks are increasingly unemployed — drifting, as every unemployed section of the working class historically has, into petty crime and pilfering. The colony areas are the incipient basis for an increasingly restless and alienated population. This is where the crisis bites. Practically, these areas have to be **policed** with increasing strictness. But, also, the crisis has to be explained. Ideologically it has to be dealt with, contained and managed. Blacks become the bearers, the signifiers, of the crisis of British society in the 70s: racism is its 'final solution'. The class which is called upon to bear the brunt of a deepening economic crisis is divided and segmented — along racial lines. If racism had not existed as a plausible way in which the underclasses of society could have 'lived through' the crisis of the British social formation in the 1970s, it would surely have had to be invented then.

This is not a crisis **of** race. But race punctuates and periodizes the crisis. Race is the lens through which people come to perceive that a crisis is developing. It is the framework through which the crisis is experienced. It is the means by which the crisis is to be resolved — 'send it away'. It is the means through which the movement, at the level of politics and the state, is 'pioneered' towards what we must now regard as a quite exceptional movement and form: a movement which comes to rely much less than it had in the previous two decades on the construction of consensus, and much more on the law and on coercion. Race is the sound in the working of the society, or a social order, which is girding itself up to iron times, preparing to take tough measures for tough circumstances. It is, above all, the language of racism which has the effect of connecting the 'crisis of the state' **above** with the state of the streets, and little old ladies hustled off pavements in the depths down **below**. That is to say, it makes the 'crisis' real for ordinary people. It's like hanging, it 'wonderfully concentrates the popular mind'.

In his famous speech at Northfield during the 1970 election, Mr Powell had warned of what he called the 'invisible enemy within' — students 'destroying' universities and 'terrorising' cities, 'bringing down' governments; of the power of the form of the modern mob — the demonstration — making 'governments tremble'; the success of disorder, 'deliberately fomented for its own sake', the near-destruction of civil government in Northern Ireland; and the accumulation of what he called 'further combustible material' of 'another kind'. The problem, however, he asserted, has been 'miscalled race'. Race is being used, he suggested, to mystify and confuse the people. The real target is not race. It is the great liberal conspiracy, inside government and the media, which has held ordinary people up to ransom, making them fearful to speak the truth for the fear of being called 'racialist' and 'literally made to say that black is white'. It is race — but now as the pivot of this 'process of brainwashing by repetition of manifest absurdities'; it is race as a 'secret weapon', 'depriving them of their wits and convincing them that what they thought right was wrong'; in short, it's race as the conspiracy of silence against the silent and long-suffering majorities — the white majorities. This is the language of an authentic, regressive, national populism. It is articulated, of course, through the potent metaphors of race. Its echo, of course, lives on, expanded and amplified in the panic climate of 1978 — even if the terms are different, the rhetoric less compelling, and the accent more 'refined'. Populist racism is no longer the preserve and prerogative of a minority which is prophesying in the wilderness. It has become 'naturalized — the normal currency of exchange at the heart of the political culture about this question, and it can be read, any day, on the front page of the *Daily Mail.*

I have said that the emergence of an ideology of indigenous racism has often assumed what I called the form of a 'moral panic'. I want now to say a word about what a moral panic is and how I think it operates. Moral panics have been defined as follows, in a quotation from Stan Cohen's book *Folk Devils and Moral Panics,*[2] which is a study of mods and rockers in the 1960s.

'Societies', he says, *'appear every now and then to be subject to periods of moral panic. A condition, an episode, person or group of persons emerges to become defined as a threat to societal values and interests; its nature is presented in a stylized and stereo-typical fashion by the mass media; the moral barricades are manned by editors and bishops and politicians and other right-thinking people; socially accredited experts pronounce their diagnoses and solutions; ways of coping are evolved, or more often resorted to; the condition then disappears or submerges or deteriorates and becomes more visible. Sometimes the panic is passed over and forgotten, but at other times it has more serious and long-term repercussions and it might produce changes in legal and social policy or even in the way in which the societies conceive themselves'.* That definition, which is about youth and the way in which social society has reacted to the problems of youth in the 50s and 60s, could, I think, with very little alteration, be extended to the emergence in Britain of an indigenous racism. The important features of the 'moral panic', as an ideological process are these: it represents a way of dealing with what are diffuse and often unorganised social fears and anxieties. It deals with those fears and anxieties, not by addressing the real problems and conditions which underlie them, but by projecting and displacing them on to the identified social group. That is to say, the moral panic crystallizes popular fears and anxieties which have a real basis and by providing them with a simple, concrete, identifiable, simple, social object, seeks to resolve them. Around these stigmatized groups or events, a powerful and popular groundswell of opinion can often be mustered. It is a groundswell which calls, in popular accents, on the 'authorities' to take controlling action. 'Moral panics' therefore, frequently serve as ways of pioneering practices by the state which, in the end, increase effective social control, but with this difference: it is the movement towards a closing of a society which has the popular legitimacy, which has been able to win popular consent. That is to say, the moral panic is one of the forms in which a largely voiceless and essentially powerless section of the community can draw attention and give expression to their concrete problems and call for remedies and solutions. Thus, the language of moral panics, whether they're about race or youth, provide a set of simple explanatory terms. They provide a popular vocabulary of discontent and are the way in which the people address themselves to their problems and address those problems to those in power. They consequently also provide vocabularies and motive and action through which the people themselves can be addressed. And in formal democracies, where policies, especially when they are tough and constraining, have to be given popular legitimacy and consent, 'moral panics' can also sometimes provide the basis by which a kind of authoritarianism can be **constructed**.

We have, undoubtedly, in the late 60s and 70s, seen both parts of this process in operation. We have seen a distinctive movement towards a movement of closure and of control in the state, and the complementary construction of popular authoritarian ideologies of which racism is in my view, only one. Both have operated, of course, in the condition of a deepening economic recession. Though they are not reducible to the economic level, they are quite specific ideological processes. They need to be understood as such. Indeed, whichever political party has been in power and in control of the management of the crisis, the ideological terrain has undoubtedly been defined and colonized through this shift into authoritarianism.

So we can find it in the general assault on the concept of welfare, the militant advocacy of the virtues of social competition and of what are now called 'social marked values'. We find it in the assault on 'progressive' and 'comprehensive' trends in education, in the call for a 'return' to standards and to the traditional curriculum, and to discipline and authority in the classroom and, if necessary, to corporal punishment and the cane. We can find it in the aggressive defence of traditional moral standards and values and the traditional family and the opposition to every tentative movement of liberalization in the moral and sexual area and, above all, in the position of women. We find it in the 'moral backlash' itself, in the summons to worship at the traditional shrines and pieties.

Race is only one of the elements in this wider ideological crusade to 'clean up' Britain, to roll up the map of progressive liberalism and to turn the clock of history back to the times when the world was 'safe for ordinary Englishmen'. And parties in power, of whatever political complexion, which fondly imagine that they are in command of the forces and tendencies which are moving and shaping popular consciousness, and do not remotely appear to understand the degree to which they are not riding, but **ridden**, well they too are driven and directed by this wave. The historical stage, the political agenda, has been set, quite often, in the 70s, in the ideological terrain specifically, and the political and economic forces have followed in the channels which they have opened up.

I want to insist that race is *one* element of this crisis which belongs to the British social formation as a whole and that it has been a leading, indeed a key, element in the process. It is grounded in natural, obvious, visible, biological facts. It is a way of drawing distinctions and of making differences in practices which are perfectly 'natural', which are given, which are universal, which we are told all of us house a trace of. It has, for instance, become an acceptable explanation of some features of racism in the British police, in their interactions with the black population, that after all they are only a cross-section of the 'great British public'. That is to say, there is bound 'naturally' to be a due proportion of 'racists' among them. Race provides precisely the set of simplifications which makes it possible to deal and explain troubling developments of that kind. After all, who now wants to begin to explore and unravel the complex tissue of political and economic forces which have created and sustained the poverty of inner-urban working class districts? Who has time for that complicated exercise, especially if it requires us to trace and make connections between things which it is better to keep apart? Above all, if there is a simple, obvious and more natural explanation at hand? Of course they are 'poor' because the **blacks** are **here**. That is not a logical proposition, but ideologies do not function by logic — they have logic of their own. Race has provided, in periods of crisis and upheaval, precisely such a self-justifying circle of explanations.

I want to end by insisting on that. I want to insist that racism is not a set of false pleas which swim around in the head. They're not a set of mistaken perceptions. They have their basis in real material conditions of existence. They arise because of the concrete problems of different classes and groups in the society. Racism represents the attempt ideologically to construct those conditions, contradictions and problems in such a way that they can be dealt with and deflected in the same moment. That instead of confronting the conditions and problems which indeed do face white and black in the urban areas, in an economy in recession, they can be projected away through race. Until the specificity of a British racism which has those real authentic material conditions at its roots, which does indeed address the real problems of the people, which is not a set of phoney conspiracies generated in the heads of the ruling class, which has a real life at the base of the society — until we can confront a racism which is specific in that sense, we haven't a hope, in my view, of turning the tide.

References
[1] *Black and White: Negro and English Society, 1555-1945.* Published by Allen Lane, 1973.
[2] *Folk Devils and Moral Panics: Creation of Mods and Rockers.* Published by MacGibbon and Kee, 1972.

Asians in Britain: Problem or Opportunity?
Dr Bhikhu Parekh
Senior Lecturer in Politics at the University of Hull

In this lecture I intend to discuss the life of the Asian immigrant settled in Britain. For reasons I'll be discussing later, I shall begin with an extremely brief and rather tentative sketch of the historical encounters between Britain and the colonies. I shall then describe in some detail, the experiences of, and the differences between, the first and second generation immigrants. Since the structures of these experiences are determined to a large extent by the wider British society, I shall then consider the attitude of the British to the colonial minority. In the final part I shall explain why I take the view that the contemporary debate on race relations leaves a great deal to be desired, and then I shall suggest the lines along which the place of the coloured minorities should be discussed.

Relations between individuals are determined by two basic facts about human beings. First, each human being is unique and has his own distinctive way of thinking, feeling, judging and determining his responses to those around him. Second, human beings are born into and belong to specific economic, political, cultural, religious and other groups. They belong to upper, middle and working classes; they are Indians, Pakistanis, British, Americans or West Indians; they are Hindus, Muslims, Christians or Jews; and so on. As such they perceive and react to each other not merely as unique beings but as members of specific groups. Their relations are structured and mediated by the wider relations between the groups to which they belong. Joe, a Christian, does not relate to Joseph, a Jew, as one unique individual to another. They approach each other against the background of the history of their respective groups, and are profoundly influenced by their historical memories and the patterns of relationship resulting from centuries of interaction. In short, every interpersonal relationship is also an inter-group relationship, and every inter-group relationship can only be actualised and expressed in an interpersonal relationship. Liberal social theorists generally view interpersonal relations as products of conscious choices by the individuals involved and ignore the elements of historical and structural mediation. Marxists, structuralists and functionalists make the opposite mistake of ignoring the ways in which individuals can, in their interpersonal relations, modify the influence of historical and structural constraints. Although I cannot argue the point here, I wish to maintain that both historical and structural constraints on the one hand and individual choices on the other must be taken into account in any explanation of interpersonal relations, that the degree to which determined individuals can modify historical and structure constraints is rather limited, and that therefore we must never lose sight of these historical constraints and patterns if we are to understand the relations between specific groups of men.

If what I've said is correct, the relations between the Asian immigrants and the native Britons can be best understood against the background of their colonial encounter and the unequal economic and political power relationship generated by it. Colonialism had two dimensions, namely economic and cultural. By its very nature, colonialism was a master-servant relationship and fundamentally exploitative in nature. Colonies were largely suppliers of raw material and consumers of imperial industrial products; and the native bourgeoisie, such as it was, played a subordinate role to imperial interests. Not only did colonies remain poor, but also their economic systems, closely tied to that of Britain, were seriously distorted. The simple fact that even after decades and, in some cases, centuries of colonial rule they were still very poor and undeveloped when granted independence is a sufficient proof of this.

The second, cultural, factor turned economic subservience into cultural and moral inferiority. A nation cannot subjugate others without convincing itself that it is right to do so, and that it is gifted with qualities the others lack. The British drew a fairly neat contrast between themselves and their subject races. They ascribed to themselves qualities the natives lacked, and declared themselves free from those the latter seemed to possess in plenty. Such a contrastive mode of self-definition meant that the British eliminated from their self-image a large class of qualities and attributes. The natives were emotional, like women and children; by contrast, the British had to be unflappable. The natives were spontaneous; by contrast the British were cool and calculating; the natives were tribal and depended on others; by contrast a Briton stood on his own two feet — and so on. The familiar bourgeois liberal view of man, suitably sharpened during the colonial encounter, gave rise to a view of man that became the standard by which the British judged themselves and other societies, and worked out a neat scale of humanity. Since the standard was derived from their own modes of thought and life, the British naturally found that of all the peoples they most closely approximated it and accordingly placed themselves at the top of the human hierarchy. The continentals, who were internally graded, came to be placed below the English. The Asians, pejoratively called the Asiatic people, were placed third, and the Africans were placed the lowest. Since different peoples occupied different rungs of the human hierarchy, different values were placed upon them. For example, the lowest value was placed upon the life of an African, who could therefore be bought and sold like chattel. By contrast the value of an

Englishman's life was the highest. By its very nature, the English brand of racism could not be aggressive and militant like the French, nor strident and murderous like the German, for these qualities were incongruous with the image of man underlying English racism. The English racism was calm, arrogant, secure in its self-righteousness, and self-confident.

Non-European societies found these ideological definitions of man very difficult to resist. No doubt, there was some resistance and scepticism in the beginning, but it collapsed before systematic British indoctrination carefully carried out by educational, legal, political and economic means. To be fair, the natives themselves were sometimes a willing party. They were impressed by British self-confidence, power and energy, and were only too eager to imbibe the ways of thought and life that had made these possible. So gradually the black man began to internalise British values, and with these, the British image of him. The white man said that the black man's religion was superstitious, that his morality was primitive, his social and legal institutions backward and his traditions uncouth, and the black man agreed. The white man said that the native was uncivilised and barbaric, and the black man, again, agreed. The white man said that the native could become fully human only if he got Westernised, and the native concurred. The bewitched native, judging himself on the basis of European values and ideals, felt that he could not respect himself if he failed to live up to them. Since these values were not an outgrowth from, and therefore unsuited to, his temperament and background, be naturally found it difficult fully to live up to them. However hard he tried, he failed, thus reinforcing his own and his master's belief that he was naturally, inherently, an inferior creature. Bemused into believing that he was less gifted and therefore less of a man than the white man, he felt a profound sense of inferiority in his presence, and could not feel or act like an equal in his relations with him; the white man, for his part, could not see how he could accept a man of proven inferiority as his equal. Once the native's soul was conquered, the stage was set for the racist belief that he was lacking in those essential qualities that made a man fully human.

Since the term racism has been used rather indiscriminately and since I shall use it in this paper, let me begin by explaining what I mean by it. Racism is not the same as racial prejudice. Prejudice is a partial rejection of a man on the basis of his real or supposed specific or specifiable characteristics. A white man may be prejudiced against a black man because he thinks he is lazy, sexy, dirty, mean, unclean, unintelligent, and so on, even as a black man might be prejudiced against a white man because in his view he is selfish, inhuman, merciless, devious, emotionally undeveloped, and the like. Since prejudice is based on some assumed characteristic of the victim, it can be countered by showing that he does not in fact possess this characteristic, or that it is not really obnoxious, or that he can be helped to get rid of it. Racism belongs to a very different category. It involves a total refusal to accept the victim as a full human being entitled to the respect due to a fellow human being, and implies that his belonging to a particular race has so corrupted his humanity that he belongs to an entirely different species.

As is obvious, I do not use the term racist to refer to a man who holds that mankind is divisible into different races, each one distinctive, without drawing any moral and political conclusion from this, nor do I use the term to refer to a man who holds that some races are intellectually or in some other specific respect inferior to others, since they well might be, and the person holding this view might go on to advocate policies designed to remove their inferiority. I use the term racist to refer to a man or a body of men who hold that some races, however identified, are inferior not in this or that respect but *qua men*, and that therefore their interests and feelings do not deserve to be regarded as equally important with those of the other so-called superior race. As I use the term, racism refers not merely to a body of beliefs but also and primarily to the type of conduct it generates. Thus a person who believes that the coloured people are intellectually inferior, and then goes on to propose discrimination in their favour is not a racist, but he **is** racist who, on the basis of this belief, argues that they should therefore be treated as less than fully human and may be exploited with a clear conscience.

During the colonial era, immigration was almost entirely one-sided. The British emigrated to different parts of the world. They were not invited by the natives; they simply stormed their way into other people's lands, and turned them into either colonies over which they ruled or their new homelands where they settled. They justified their right to settle in these countries or to rule over them on the ground that they had conquered them or, what is extraordinary, that they had 'discovered' them. Although the Indians and the Aborigines had lived in America and Australia respectively for centuries, the Europeans maintained and still maintain that they 'discovered' the two countries, the underlying assumption being that although people had already been living in these countries, the latter did not really exist until the Europeans graced them with their presence. Like the Christian God, the Europeans created them *ex nihilo* and conferred existence on them.

Even after decolonisation, the British continued to emigrate, largely to countries which they claimed to have 'discovered'. Decolonisation, however, introduced new elements into this pattern of international and essentially one-sided migration. It now became a two-way process, and while hitherto capital had migrated abroad, now it was labour's turn. In the 1950s, first the West Indians, and then the Asians began to come to Britain. Although there were murmurs of protest, Britain badly needed their labour, and allowed them in without undue restriction.

Asian immigrants came to Britain for a variety of reasons. Some had tied themselves too closely to British rule, and could not survive its disappearance. This was true of the Anglo-Indians and the Parsees, as well as of the East African Asians. Some others had acquired love of the British way of life and felt that they would be happier in Britain than in their own countries whose physiognomy was bound to alter under indigenous rule. Many, however, immigrated because, like the British and partly because of the British encouragement, they had developed a tradition of migration in search of better prospects. They came to Britain not immediately after the independence of their countries, but several years later when the economic structure of their countries, gravely distorted and lamentably undeveloped under British rule, offered them little hope for the future. According to the 1971 census the total number of immigrants born in the New Commonwealth was 1,157,170; i.e. about 2.1% of the total population. About half of them come from the Indian sub-continent, under a third from the West Indies, and the rest from Cyprus, Africa and other countries. The total immigrant population is around two millions; just under half born in Britain and likely to constitute between 3 and 3½% of the total population by the end of the century.

Some Asians came to Britain with their families. Many more, however, came alone in the hope that they could save enough to call their families later. Nearly all of them originally came here determined to spend no more than between five and seven years and then to return permanently to their native lands. However, they soon realised that their plans had to be revised. Many found that it took them two to three years to save up the money needed to call their families. It generally took them several weeks to find jobs; the jobs were low paid; they were usually the first to be retrenched in times of recession and unemployment; and they had to send substantial portions of their meagre savings back home to maintain their wives and children as well as their parents and relatives. They found, further, that even after they had managed to save enough to call their family, they had to wait on average between two and three years before the British Government would allow their families to enter the country. In short, they had to wait five to seven years before they could even be united with their families in Britain. And so the initial five to seven years stint became a ten to fifteen year period. As they lived here for ten to fifteen years they found that further difficulties had cropped up. By the time they had spent fifteen years here, many of them are well into their middle age. A return to their country at this stage is economically disastrous. People retire in India much earlier than in Britain, and middle aged men have little chance of finding jobs. They cannot set up new businesses either, for their absence abroad has deprived them of influential contacts so necessary to obtain loans, import-export licences, and the like. They must therefore stay yet longer and save yet more so, that they can live in India on their savings alone.

There is also yet another complicating factor. The longer they stay in Britain, the more Anglicised their children become, and the less they are able to fit into the Indian education system. A return to India is therefore a severe wrench for them. And so the parents decide to stay on until their children complete their education. The plan to stay for fifteen to twenty years is therefore revised yet again. They must now stay for at least twenty five years, the initial period of five or so years when they were on their own and eighteen or so years for their children to finish their schooling. By the time they have spent twenty five years in Britain, they have, however, grown old, have very few relatives and friends still left in India and have been out of India too long to fit in in ease. What is more, their children, to whom India is only a name and Britain their home, resolutely refuse to return to India. The Asian immigrants are predictably frightened and bewildered. They are haunted by a sense of impending tragedy and a growing feeling of meaninglessness. They have been caught up in a cycle of circumstances from which they cannot break out. As several Indians in their early sixties put it to me, they cannot bear the thought of getting old and dying in this 'cold and alien land', and yet they cannot see how they can avoid this. They have tried various methods to ease their predicament. Some of them 'import' spouses for their children from India in the twin hope that this will enable them to establish a network of relations in India and to forge links between their children and India. Their efforts have, however, run into opposition not only from their children but even more from the British Government which for strange reasons, is set against allowing fiances and fiancees to settle in Britain. Unable to return for good, and unwilling to stay on, some of them have taken to commuting between India and Britain, spending a few months there and a few here. Whether they can for long sustain such an expensive practice, and whether the practice will become a future trend is difficult to say.

The life of the first generation Asian immigrant in Britain was, and is, sad and depressing. He did not, and even now does not, speak English. He was not used to the mores and practices of an industrialised society. His presence was resented, and he suffered racialist insults and indignities. He was denied a decent house and a job commensurate with his abilities. He was often not promoted to a higher position. All these have been systematically studied and analysed in PEP and other reports, although even they fail to bring out the full extent of immigrant suffering. The immigrants were able to endure the hardships and survive for a variety of reasons. They looked upon themselves as immigrants and developed what I might call a 'guest complex'. The complex consists in feeling that they are outsiders in Britain, that they should therefore feel a sense of gratitude to the 'host' country, thankfully accept whatever is made available to them, and deserve well of their hosts by good and orderly behaviour and by making only minimal demands on the nation's resources. The first generation immigrant draws a fairly neat distinction between his

Janma-Bhumi, the land of birth, and *Karma-bhumi*, the land of efforts. He is in Britain to better his and his family's material prospects. He has little love for the country, has limited sympathy and contact with its culture, and looks forward to a day when he can comfortably retire or at least find permanent rest in his native country. He therefore only asks to be left alone. His native country is his constant frame of reference. He compares his lot with that of his relatives back home, calculates his savings in terms of rupees, and is content to know that he is better off than them. This is why, as several surveys have shown, the average Asian does not consider his house or conditions of work to be sub-standard, although they are such by British standards. Again, since his attitudes and feelings towards the British were formed in the heyday of colonialism, the first generation Asian retains a good deal of the colonial native's sense of inferiority, and feels nervous and timid in his relations with white Britons. He walks in the shadow and close to the wall. He avoids confrontation, 'plays dumb' and swallows his pride.

The second generation Asian's attitude is rather different. Although he is often described as a second generation immigrant, the Asian child feels that he is not at all an immigrant, but a first generation Brown Briton. As such he is free from the 'guest complex'. He does not think that he should feel grateful for the privilege of being allowed to live in Britain. Britain is his home. He belongs to it, and it to him, just as much as it belongs to his white compatriots. Consequently, he does not feel the need to justify his existence, that is, to prove that he is a worthy member of the country, and makes claims on the country his parents never thought of making. Further, unlike them, his standards of comparison and points of reference are drawn from Britain. He judges his job, house, income, opportunities, and the like by British standards, and demands equality with his white compatriots. Unlike his parents who, under a mistaken sense of gratitude and insecurity did not press their demands for justice and fair play and either relied on the whites to fight for them or wallowed in self-pity, the second generation immigrant insists upon fighting his battle himself. Although the incidents of blatant discriminaton and crude racial insults have somewhat diminished over the years, the level of expectation and the sensitivity to discrimination have increased; and therefore, although the second generation immigrant is, objectively speaking, marginally better off than his parents, he feels discriminated against far more acutely than they did. Unlike them, his image of the British is based not on colonial experience but on his day to day contacts. The British are not, for him, distant and aloof demi-gods, but creatures of flesh and blood with whom he competes and whom he sometimes excels in matters relating to jobs, women, education and the like. He is therefore free from his parents' deep-seated feeling of inferiority and insecurity in his dealings with the native British, and feels much less inhibited in standing up for his rights.

The differences between the attitudes, experiences and frameworks of reference between the first and second generation Asians have naturally generated tensions between them. The tensions are expressed, interpreted and dealt with differently in different Asian families depending on their degrees of Anglicisation, periods of stay in Britain, their proximity to other immigrant families, and the like. Nevertheless hardly any Asian family is entirely free from them. The second generation Asian is critical of his parents' orthodoxy, and seeks liberalisation of traditional Asian customs, especially those related to sex. He also finds his parents too meek and submissive for his taste. He disapproves of their lack of political self-reliance and their continuing dependence on the white liberals to fight their battles for them. He is critical, too, of the traditional Asian leadership which is predominantly middle-aged and drawn either from business or professions, especially the medical. The second generation Asian leadership is generally young and drawn from the working or lower middle classes. Above all, unlike the first generation Asians, the second generation is impressed by and seeks close contact with its West Indian counterpart.

The conflict between the immigrant and the British culture has predictably generated various kinds of conflict, both at the personal and impersonal level. These conflicts have all been mistakenly classified under the catch-all diagnostic label of 'cultural conflict'. Every time a child displays insecurity, or behavioural maladjustment or appears aggressive, he is diagnosed by social workers, head teachers, judges and others as a victim of cultural conflict. And the experts fall over each other trying to find for it a non-existent answer. What is called cultural conflict includes a wide variety of situations, some of which cannot be subsumed under its capacious umbrella. Sometimes, so-called cultural conflict is not more than a generation conflict endemic in all societies. Sometimes it is little more than a rejection of a specific cultural custom, for example, arranged marriages, rather than the immigrant's parental culture as a whole. Sometimes is is a conflict not between two cultures but between colour and culture, as when a black child has fully adopted the British way of life but because of his colour, is not accepted as British by the white community. Some of the acute cases of the so-called cultural conflict arise because of the sense of self-rejection generated by the white society's denigration of the immigrant's culture. Often the dominant white culture encourages an immigrant child, by subtle and not so subtle means, to despise his own culture. He then develops an attitude of self-rejection, self-contempt, and with it, a contempt for his parents. There are countless cases where a child of four or five calls his parents 'you damn Pakis' and then runs away in tears; where girls and boys of ten and eleven are ashamed of walking in the streets with their parents or of being heard speaking in their own languages; where adolescents describe themselves not as Indians or Pakistanis but as

Mexicans or Italians, as they did in the early sixties. Again there are cases of children struggling to wash themselves white, persuading their mothers not to wear saris, asking their parents to give them new names, not inviting their friends home lest they should find out that they are Indians or Pakistanis, and the like. Many of these cases are extremely tragic and cannot be solved unless Britain recognises itself as a multi-cultural society and takes firm and positive steps to encourage a sense of positive identity in its cultural minorities.

Now, the cases of cultural conflict properly so called, are those where a child feels sympathetic to both the British and the Asian cultures and is wracked by their conflicting demands. Such cases, although dramatised by the media, are relatively few. In a population of a million Asians, there are not even a hundred cases of children leaving their parental homes in anger and frustration. This is a much smaller number than that to be found in British society at large and in India. What is more, some of these cases of revolt are largely symbolic, intended to dramatise their frustrations and to exert pressure on their parents, rather than to effect a permanent break. This is evident in the fact that most of these young boys and girls eventually return to their parents.

There are several reasons why the so-called cultural conflict is less widespread and takes less explosive forms than is generally supposed. First, the second generation Asian immigrant is far less Westernised than is generally realised by others, and even by him. His Westernisation does not generally extend beyond his mannerisms, language, dress, food habits, style of life and the like, and rarely penetrates his innermost attitude to life. Like his parents, his innermost or primary identity is essentially Asian. He remains rooted in his parental culture and imbibes only as much of the British way of life as is necessary to help him get by in the British society without appearing odd and awkward. Two recent surveys, one by Dr Anwar and the other by Mr Taylor bear this out. If we took attitude to marriage as the index to a person's degree of westernisation, it is striking that in Dr Anwar's survey, 78% of the young Asians believe that they should marry within their own communities, and 67% of them even approved of arranged, or rather parentally guided, marriages. Mr Taylor's findings point in the same direction.

The second reason for the containment of the cultural conflict has to do with the structure of the Asian family. The Asian family is extremely close-knit and characterised by considerable emotional inter-dependence. It is almost like a living organism whose members constitute its interdependent limbs. They share in common their triumphs and tragedies, joys and sorrows, and depend on each other for guidance, encouragement and inspiration. As a result the young grow up lacking an atomic and exclusive notion of the self, and are unable to exist outside the supportive relationship of the family. They may intellectually subscribe to Western values but their emotional being is almost utterly un-Western. This diminishes their capacity to rebel; and if they do rebel, the rebellion is largely symbolic. Furthermore, the relationship between parents, especially the father and the children, is characterised by a fascinating blend of authority and vulnerability. At one level the father is remote and aloof and is expected to be obeyed without demur. At another level, he is dependent on his children, freely acknowledges his failings and deficiences, and expects to be protected. His children therefore feel both deferential and protective towards him. Consider the following remark by Lalu, a Sikh adolescent in one of Mulk Raj Anand's novels:

> '*Lalu was taken aback by the onslaught even though he had expected it. One part of him longed to struggle. But the feeling of docility and respect that had been inculcated in him since birth made him dumb and unresisting, though he smouldered with rage and self-pity.*'

Or take again the following fairly typical remark, quoting from Mr Taylor's *The Half-Way Generation:*

> '*Our religion has everything to do with family, I mean religion says that we should live together. This is one of the biggest things, respect your elders. I've been brought up to this. My brothers they can come in the house, say something — I've got to do it, whether I like it or not. Say for example I refused him once, which I did. This was when I was working at the market, and he just turned round and slapped us in the face. I was 19 then. See if I had been an English lad myself, I know this, he would have turned round and hit him one. But not me ... I just turned, started working. To my point of view this is respect. See I respected him in front of all those people. But I know I went down. I was ashamed for myself. But I mean he realised it afterwards, what he had done wrong.*'

Finally, the Indian family is characterised by a spirit of accommodation, generated and sustained by the resolute desire of its members to preserve the integrity and prestige of the family. If one of its young members persisted in a demand unacceptable to his or her parents, they would more often than not give in, provided of course that he or she has adroitly manipulated the emotional and power relations prevailing within the family. If they do not, he or she can threaten to revolt, and that usually does the trick. Even in the most serious cases of inter-caste marriages, parents usually give in either before or soon after the marriage. A dozen such marriages that I know were all initially opposed by the parents concerned. Within less than a year, the parents had become reconciled to all but one. Consider the following fairly typical remark:

> '*It caused a lot of upset in the family. This is it. He was thrown out of it in fact. But he's come into it again. See, we brought him in, because we knew if we threw him out, what will he do? He'll just go the English way. We're finished with him, you see, for the rest of our lives. We won't get to know his children. They won't get to know us. I mean then he will start up on his own — set up family somewhere else. We will*

never get in contact with each other. So we brought her and him into our family. Now they are part of us.'

Even as the second generation Asian immigrant has not yet broken out of his parents' traditional culture, he has also failed to break out of some of the attitudes their parents inherited from the British in the colonial period. This is evident in his relations with his West Indian counterpart. At one level he admires the West Indian youth and feels inferior to him. He is impressed by the latter's lack of inhibition and repression, defiance of both white and black establishment, ability to stand up to his elders, his extrovert gaiety, group solidarity, capacity to attract public attention, his aggressiveness, and the like. At the same time, he is too firmly rooted in the Asian culture to strike up a meaningful relationship with him. He is also critical of the West Indian's alleged lack of respect for elders, his political impatience, social intolerance, his alleged lack of commercial skill and ambition and drive. Although the second generation Asian has copied some of the superficial mannerisms of his West Indian counterpart — his defiant walk, colloquial expressions, snapping of fingers, habit of moving in groups, anti-authority gestures and jokes — there is little meaningful contact between the two. What is more, whenever the Asian youth have employed their West Indian mannerisms and tactics in an Asian context, they have provoked bewilderment and resentment among their elders. Unless they are suitably Asianised, the West Indian influences are unlikely to last long.

The Asian Youth's attitude to its West Indian counterpart is, no doubt, undergoing a change, partly because they are beginning to discover that their problems are basically the same, and partly under the political compulsions of the changing racial climate in Britain. Until a couple of years ago the British society directed its animosity towards the Blacks and appeared tolerant of the Asians, who therefore did not feel threatened. In recent years the roles have been reversed and the Asian has become the target. For the past two years more West Indians have been leaving the country than coming in. By contrast, the number of Asian dependents knocking at the doors is still considerable. Further, unlike the West Indians, the Asians have their own distinct culture which they demand to be taught in schools. They are therefore seen to threaten Britain's alleged cultural homogeneity and to force her to become a multicultural society. Realising that they are now the targets, the Asians are beginning to explore ways to combine forces with the West Indians.

I have so far discussed some of the problems faced by the first and second generation Asian immigrants, and the patterns of interaction between the two generations as well as between them and the West Indians. Neither the problems nor the patterns of interaction exist in a vacuum. They are created and shaped by the wider context in which they occur. It is to the examination of this context that I now wish to turn.

I referred earlier to the racist scale of humanity developed during the colonial era. The racism developed during this era did not disappear when the ex-colonial subjects began to arrive in Britain. To be fair, they were not exposed to the ugly forms of racism to which they and their ancestors were subjected by their British colonial masters. Britain has always maintained an important distinction between domestic and colonial policy. Within Britain a tradition of relatively humane liberalism was maintained and insisted upon, whereas the ugly forms of racism were allowed to be maintained in the relations between the British rulers and their colonial subjects. This distinction is maintained even now. The laws passed by the British Parliament have been, relatively speaking, free from crude racism, whereas the dirty task of operating a rather racist immigration policy has been assigned to the Entry Certificate Officers in British diplomatic outposts abroad.

Although less crude and ugly, the racist attitudes developed during the imperialist era did not vanish simply because the colonial natives, now settled in Britain, were fully fledged British citizens rather than colonial subjects. They have continued to dominate the white society's approach to the immigrants. Since this has been abundantly made clear by various PEP, CRC and other reports,[1] I shall not elaborate upon the subject. What I'd like to do is to point to a relatively new feeling of resentment against the coloured immigrants that has developed over the past two decades and given the racist attitude a rather peculiar orientation. The feeling of resentment has never clearly been expressed, but it is fairly powerful and widely held. It can be best described as follows: the coloured immigrant should not really be here, he does not belong here and is an undesirable nuisance. He stealthily sneaked into the country when the nation was not alert and is intent upon smuggling many many more 'of his kind' in under one pretext or another. The nation should therefore vigilantly watch his every movement and every step if it is not to be tricked again by his wily manoeuvres; it should also guard its frontiers day and night, and man its overseas outposts by tough officers capable of detecting and resisting the immigrants' most devious ploys. The combination of racism and resentment has given rise to a rather dangerous attitude to the coloured immigrants. Once the immigrants are transformed into dark thieves who entered the country in the darkness of the night, they are almost automatically placed outside the pale of civilised behaviour. Thieves are dishonourable men and cannot expect to be treated honourably. Similarly, once we look upon the immigrants as men who entered the country when the nation was inflicted by its apparently chronic state of absent-mindedness, we can with a clear conscience send them back to their countries, now that the nation, thanks to Mr Powell's noisy and strident alarm bell, is fully awake. And again, once we come to believe that the immigrants have tricked the nation into letting them in, by first coming singly and then insisting bringing in their wives and children, we feel it proper to show equal deviousness and cunning in our relations with them. I need hardly say that the feeling of resentment, of being tricked, hurt and outsmarted, which has really no basis in facts, has become a rather convenient ideological device and a subtle psychological defence-mechanism by which to cover up the full horror of discriminatory policies and to put the nation's conscience at ease. Mr Powell's strength is derived from, among other things, his ability to play the role of the ideologue with considerable skill and subtlety. He placates the racist lobby by his racist proposals, and puts the non-racist conscience at ease by arguing that the dishonourable and devious immigrants deserve every bit of the treatment meted out to them.

In talking about racist resentment, I did not at all wish to suggest that Britain is a racist society, nor that every Briton is a racist. Such a suggestion would be utterly false and grossly unfair. When all is said and done, Britain is one of the most decent and civilised societies in the world, and is characterised by a considerable sense of fairness and humanity. What is more, there are powerful sections of public opinion who would do everything in their power to rectify cases of racial unjustice when brought to their attention. My point is basically this. The sections of public opinion that have hitherto had the greatest impact have been racist. They have dictated the terms of the public debate and the basic outlines of the government policies. The non-racist sections have been able to do little more than moderate the tide of racism and, on occasion, to extract a few concessions. The racist sections have had this degree of impact for a number of reasons. First, they were in the business long before the non-racist sections appeared on the scene, and have over the years articulated the terms of the debate, formulated the question to be debated, and determined the basic framework within which the debate takes place. Second, they have exploited the misconceived sense of resentment shared by all sections of the community, and thereby emasculated the impact of the non-racist criticisms. Third, the racist sections have skilfully selected and dramatised cases of abuse, presented their views with passion and pseudo-prophetic foresight, and have created a climate in which men of good will have been led to doubt their instinct and judgement, and to wonder whether they may not be mistaken, whether there is not a danger of Britain going the way of America, and whether the immigrants may not fundamentally alter the character of the British way of life.

Whatever the explanation, the fact remains that the coloured immigrants have been subject to varying forms and degrees of discrimination and abuse. This is evident in the widespread discrimination in housing, jobs and promotions, in the persistent refusal to recognise the special and cumulative disadvantages derived from colour, in the refusal to recognize the special educational and cultural needs of immigrant children, and the like. Indeed, almost every immigrant demand for the appreciation of its distinctive problems and requirements is resented and construed as a plea for privilege. Whenever immigrants have taken their problems to them, several local councillors and Members of Parliament up and down the country have retorted that if the immigrants were not prepared to accept their lot, they should get out.

In their view the coloured immigrants cannot have problems, because they are themselves a problem. And the fact that they bring their problems to the authorities is itself a sufficient indication of the fact that they are a problem. Take a simple case. Asian immigrants have a distinct cultural heritage which they wish to preserve. Surely there is nothing wrong in their suggestion that, if not in all, then at least in these schools where they constitute over 20% of the student population, some provision should be made for the teaching of their mother tongues, history and culture, and the inclusion of their religion in the daily religious service. Such provisions not only give the immigrant pupils a positive sense of cultural identity but also, what is equally important, secure its recognition from their white peers. While some local authorities have recognized the justice of these simple demands, others have not. The following two fairly typical remarks explain why. A headmaster remarks in the School Council's Working Paper No. 50:

> *I do not consider it the responsibility of an English state school to cater for the development of cultures and customs of a foreign nature. I believe it is our duty to prepare children for citizenship in a free Christian democratic society, according to British standards and customs.*

It is interesting that the headmaster concerned cannot acknowledge the simple fact that what he calls foreign customs are not foreign customs to a sizeable section of the British Society. It is no less interesting that he cannot accept the equally obvious fact that Hindus, Muslims, Jews and others are not Christian.

Consider yet another remark, this time by the Director of a Local Education Authority in his evidence to the Parliamentary Select Committee on Race Relations and Immigration: "The general educational problems can be summarised as follows:—

(a) **Communication** — inability to speak and write English.

(b) **For Asians** — lack of cultural support at home. Of course, this is understandable, "strangers in a strange land". Their Asian culture means so much to them. However, undeniably, it makes the work of the school difficult.

(c) **For West Indians** — They present the greatest problem. They make a point of honour of learning a West Indian patois and set out deliberately to emphasise cultural differences. Therefore they produce some 80% of the discipline problems in the school. The cultural differences are most obvious in:—

1. bad time-keeping
2. lack of ambition
3. antagonism
4. a natural tendency towards violence as a solution to their problems.''

The same racist sentiment is reflected in the way immigrants are referred to in the press and in private conversations. While a white couple has a large family, immigrants only 'breed like rabbits'; while white immigrants come in large numbers, the coloured immigrants come in 'hordes and waves'; while the whites living together constitute a community, the immigrants form a 'ghetto'. When through bureaucratic stupidity an immigrant couple from Malawi was recently housed in a four-star hotel, it was not the local authority concerned but the immigrant couple that was hounded and the immigrant community as a whole made a target of racist attacks. During more or less the same period, a white couple was similarly housed in an expensive hotel by a local authority. The media knew of it, but unanimously chose to suppress the news. In short, the immigrant is constantly hounded, denigrated, depicted as a villian responsible for the nation's malaise, and burdened with a sense of guilt for disasters with which he has nothing to do. He is told that he is an intruder in another man's house, that he is a thief stealing the nation's wealth and sometimes women, that he is a parasite upon the nation's social and welfare services, that he spreads disease and insanitation and poses a moral threat to the nation's life and well-being. Indeed his breeding habits are made a subject of careful statistical analysis, and the 'smell' of his food and the way he sleeps and relaxes are considered subjects worthy of national attention.

The racist resentment is evident again in much of the current debate on race relations. How else can we explain the fact that the morally and politically outrageous notion of repatriation should be seriously debated and considered an acceptable option? To anyone endowed with even a modicum of decency, the idea cannot but appear offensive and outrageous for two very simple reasons. First, it springs from the racist belief that the coloured immigrants are inherently incapable of sharing a civilised social life in common with the whites. And second, it is an impertinent attempt to offer the immigrants sums of money if they would agree to get out of the country. That is, repatriation is a trade in men and women, a form of slavery. It is a sad reflection on the nation's morality that it should even condescend to discuss such preposterous proposals.

The same racist resentment underlies and vitiates the country's immigration policy. No one in his right mind advocates an open-door policy, or denies the nation its right to regulate and restrict the number and kind of people coming in. The point, however, is that the immigration policy has been discussed in a racist context and used as a weapon to further the racist cause. First, the restriction on immigration almost invariably relates to the coloured, and not the white, immigrants. Second, now that the primary immigration of heads of households has been reduced to a trickle, every new restriction applies to the wives and dependents of those already settled here. On what conceivable ground can we justify the belief that while a white Briton has an unhindered right to live with his wife and children, a coloured immigrant must wait two or more years and undergo considerable harassment before a tough British bureaucrat decides that his family may now be allowed to join him? And, again, on what grounds can we justify the demand that while a Briton can marry wherever and whoever he likes, an immigrant must choose his partner from within Britain? To his credit, even Mr Powell finds this offensive.

Third, what makes the current discussion of immigration particularly unacceptable is the way in which it is so often linked with good race relations in Britain. The immigrants are told that they cannot accept fairness and justice because there are too many of them, and that if they wish to be respected, they must reduce their number by such means as not calling their families, by not reproducing too fast, and by some of them agreeing to leave the country. This is surely a preposterous and unacceptable alternative. What is more, it represents an attempt both to transfer to the immigrants the entire blame for their problems, and to avoid doing anything about the immigrants' problems by turning them into problems themselves.

The racist resentment does not always take the aggressive forms discussed earlier. It may also take defensive and negative forms and is then relatively hard to detect. In a letter to *The Times* of March 17, 1973, Mr John Sparrow, until recently Master of All Souls College, Oxford, asked why it should be considered wrong or racist to want to live with one's own people and to wish to keep out men of different culture. His question, which was well-intentioned and reflected a genuine puzzle, rests on three assumptions which border on racism. First, he assumes that it was right for Britain to break open other people's doors, but not for its colonial subjects to come to Britain. Of course, what Britain has done cannot be undone, and *ex-post facto* moral judgements are of little avail. However, history cannot be judged in convenient and arbitrary terms. A nation is a historical entity, and each generation benefits from the deeds of its predecessors. One cannot therefore accept the benefits accruing from Britain's occupation of other lands, and deny their inhabitants a right to benefit from Britain. Second, when he asks why we, the British, should be criticised for wanting to live with our own people, he rather conveniently defines 'we' and 'the British' to refer only to the white Britons, and denies the black and brown Britons so much as a right to have a say in determining national policies. So as far as the black and brown Britons are concerned, they have no objection to the arrival of others of their kind. Third, if the assumption underlying the question were carried to its logical conclusion, the countries of the Third World could legitimately object to the

British settled in their midst on the ground that they represent a different culture and an alien way of life. This is a recipe for massive international expulsion and an unwitting endorsement of General Amin.

My purpose in discussing the above-mentioned examples of racism was to show that a deep-seated resentment of the coloured immigrants, and the consequent refusal to accept them as equal and rightful members of British society, permeates much of the nation's thinking today and distorts its discussion of their place in Britain. Our entire structure of political discourse has become heavily biased in favour of the racist attitude. The terms in which we describe the immigrants, the questions we ask and the assumptions we make about them — they all point in a racist direction. And consequently even the men of impeccable honour and integrity unwittingly end up supporting racist conclusions. For example, a recent BBC programme designed to discuss race-relations in Britain soon degenerated into a discussion of how best to get rid of the immigrants. The Select Committee set up to explore the ways to improve race relations ended up spending almost all its time discussing how the number of immigrants could be kept down. An immigrant couple mistakenly housed in an expensive hotel because an occasion, not for an inquiry into the administrative procedures of the local authority in question, but for an attack on the immigrants' alleged misuse of social services.

In case after case the discussion has got seriously misdirected, and betrayed an amazing incapacity to discuss the place of the immigrants in our society in fair and honourable terms. As long as we describe a group of people as immigrants, we cannot but think of them as outsiders; similarly as long as we describe them as coloured, or Britain as a 'host' society, or talk in terms of different **races**, we cannot but view the immigrants as a separate group which is somehow not an integral part of British society. Unless the white society accepts, fully and without reservation, the presence of the coloured immigrants and revises the concepts and categories in terms of which it discusses their place in it, it will, I fear, continue to alienate them and to drive them to acts of despair.

The Asian community is profoundly upset and outraged by the persistent failure of the media and the government to discuss its problems in fair and honourable terms. This is evident in the vigilante groups being formed throughout the country. It is also evident in the beliefs of the young Asians that the media and the normal channels of communication are loaded against them, and that they should take recourse to direct action. At a different level, the Asian frustrations are evident both in the report of the Birmingham Community Development Project set up by the Home Office in conjunction with the Birmingham local authority, and in the Stechford by-election earlier this year when extreme left-wing candidates campaigning on a strong anti-racialist ticket took a large part of the Asian vote. The situation is made even more critical by the fact that the unemployment among the young Asians is rising at a much faster rate than among the whites and, even, the West Indians. Such industries as the textile industry where Asians are employed in large numbers are declaring redundancies. And the market for the self-employed, where the Asians have found employment, is getting saturated. The next few years threaten to produce waves of unrest and violence.

If we wish to avoid violence and a growing sense of alienation, we must reappraise the concepts and assumptions of the current debate about the immigrants, and approach the whole question along the following lines. As a result of Britain's imperial past, we have now in our midst people of Asian and Afro-Caribbean origin. Even as the British went and still go to other countries to earn their living, these men have come to Britain. Nearly all of them have come because we need them, and indeed recruited them. All of them are here to improve their material prospects, a perfectly honourable motive. And some of them love the British way of life. For a variety of historical reasons, they suffer hardship in Britain and are caught up in a familiar cycle of cumulative disadvantage. The relatively low-paid and low-status jobs of the first generation immigrants meant for them poor and over-crowded living conditions and a depressed environment. Since their job opportunities, living conditions and educational facilities were all poor, their children grew up less well equipped than their white counterparts. As a result they are trapped in poor jobs and poor housing and are caught up in 'a vicious downward spiral of deprivation'. Some of these problems are common to the poor whites as well, whereas some others are unique to the immigrants. As a civilised nation we regret that some of our citizens have to live a wretched existence and believe that we ought to use our material and intellectual resources to raise them to a level where they can compete with others on equal terms. This requires both a positive policy of non-discrimination and policy of positive discrimination, not with a view to giving the minority a privileged status but rather to counteract the results of previous policies of discrimination.

Some of our citizens, further, have their own distinct cultural identity. While playing their full part in British society, they wish to preserve their heritage. This is an understandable desire, and it can do no harm to Britain. Indeed, as a liberal society, we value and cherish cultural diversity. Let us therefore explore what we collectively can do to enable the immigrant minority to preserve and enrich its heritage, and how we can accommodate its distinctive cultural, religious and other requirements within a general framework of national policy.

Once we approach the question along these lines, we can then ask what obstacles stand in our way. Obviously, sections of the white community are racists, or bigoted, or obtuse, or simply confused, and therefore we must explore ways to deal with these attitudes. We may find that the number of immigrants entering the country stands in our way, and therefore we should explore ways to deal with it. Since the white society would have given ample evidence of its good intentions, shown how and why the number of immigrants is a problem, and located it in a proper context, it can legitimately ask the immigrant community to cooperate with it in dealing with this problem. Again, we may find that some of the immigrants' customs and practices are unacceptable to us. We should then draw their attention to them, enter into a dialogue with them and encourage a process of internal change. In short, once we start viewing the immigrants not as immigrants, racial minorities, guests and the like, but as part of British society and deal with common problems in a spirit of good will and reciprocal obligations, we are likely to solve these far more easily and effectively and with far less ill will than at present.

We should also then be able to appreciate the magnitude of the contribution the immigrants have made and are capable of making to the creation of a materially and culturally rich Britain. The immigrants have sustained the health, transport and other services. They have been helping Britain revitalise its decaying inner cities and set up small-scale industries there. Further, the immigrants, some of whom are heirs to rich and ancient civilisations, have brought with them new capacities, sensitivities, experiences, ideas, modes of thought and habits of reflection that cannot but be beneficial to Britain.

Take, for example, the Asian doctor. At one level, he is little different from his British counterpart. At another level he is rather different. Like his compatriots, the British doctor is not used to dealing with emotional situations. When confronted with them, he either shies away, or gets too deeply involved at the personal level. This limits his relations with his patients, especially in situations of personal stress, grief or tragedy. Furthermore, he values consideration and respect rather than concern for others, and this further limits his ability to provide solace and support in times of need. The Asian doctor, on the other hand, is used to emotional situations. He is able to share others' emotions without becoming personally involved, to show sustained personal concern without losing his balance. It comes naturally to him to take personal interest in his patients without appearing artificial or obstrusive. As such he is strong in areas where the British doctor is weak, and given right conditions capable of making an important contribution to British life. What I have said about Asian doctors could just as easily be applied to Asian and West Indian academics, school teachers, nurses, businessmen, lawyers and others.

I argued earlier that under the impact of puritanism, hasty industrialisation and colonialism, the British national character has become rather impoverished. Whilst it has developed most admirable qualities of self-discipline, professionalism, self-containment, considerateness to others and respect for the law, it has failed fully to develop such other qualities as emotional warmth, psychic openness, capacity to uncoil and relax, ability to enjoy human diversity, generosity of spirit and the like. The British were not always like this. Up until the seventeenth and even eighteenth centuries, Britain was well-known in Europe for the emotional warmth, gaiety, extrovert manners and the romantic temperament of its people, and even for the quality of its food. Henry VIII was as English as Queen Victoria. If the national fascination with the former is a reliable guide, the notion seems to feel nostalgic about this type of colourful Englishman who once inhabited these islands and is today a relatively rare species. It is in this context that the immmigrants can play an important role. They possess in large measure — perhaps too large a measure — those qualities which the British have over the past two centuries suppressed — the capacity for spontaneity, generosity, warmth, affection, relaxed interpersonal relationship, and the like. If the immigrants were allowed to relax, feel at ease and be themselves rather than put on probation and made a subject of intense microscopic examination, they may, one hopes, be able to encourage the British to relax and uncoil, and perhaps bring out some of the latent qualities of British character and make Britain a much more lively and colourful place than at present.

References
See note on page 6 and pages 79-80.

Schools and Race — Professor Alan Little
Lewisham Professor of Social Administration, University of London

There's no great argument about Government policy as far as race relations are concerned — nor about what role the schools might play in terms of creating both a just and harmonious multi-racial society.

A few years ago, the Government produced a White Paper called *Racial Discrimination*, and in it they put their finger on the crucial issue of public policy. It said:

> *'It is the Government's duty to prevent morally unacceptable and socially divisive inequalities from hardening into entrenched patterns'.* It went on: *'It is inconceivable that Britain in the last quarter of the Twentieth Century, should confess herself unable to secure for a small minority of around a million and a half coloured citizens, their full and equal rights as individual men and women'.*

Now, that is the objective of Government policy: equality and harmony between the races. It seems to me that that encapsulates what policy in race relations is all about.

As far as education is concerned, the Government has been equally clear and explicit. In another White Paper the Government said:

> *'The educational service has important contributions to make to the well-being of immigrant communities in this country, and to the promotion of harmony between the different ethnic groups of which our society is now composed. This is because'* — and these are the important points — *'first, the education service has some responsibility to assist citizens of all ages to develop their ability to the full, and within that responsibility, a special obligation to children who, for one reason or another, are most at risk of not achieving their true potential. And second, education can be a potent instrument for increasing understanding and good-will between the races.'*

This is public policy. The interesting thing about it is that the Government has puts its finger on the two distinct issues for public policy. The first is: what ought Government to be doing for the majority of the population, that is, the indigenous community and its institutions, to enable them to behave in a more effective manner towards minorities? And the second one is: to what extent have racial or ethnic minorities got special educational needs? These two ideas are contained in the sentence above — the idea that the education system has a responsibility for meeting the special needs, in so far as we can identify them, of ethnic or racial minorities, and then quite separate from that, the idea that the education system has a responsibility to enable the majority community, the indigenous community, to learn, to grow up, and to live, in a multi-racial, and hopefully harmonious and tolerant, society.

Some people would argue that the second policy objective (helping the indigenous) is the crucial one, because the problems of race relations are problems essentially of the majority. After all, they argue, it's the majority that's prejudiced, that discriminates and is hostile to minorities. It is the institutions for the majority, in this case the schools, that have been unwilling or unable to respond effectively to the minorities, and therefore, it's changes in the majority and support for those changes that's the crucial problem. I think there's a great deal in this argument. There's no doube that there's a great deal of discrimination going on in employment, in housing, and also —and I'll get onto this later — within the schools. I don't accept, however, that that is the crucial problem we should be addressing now. To use the language of priorities rather than diagnosis, it seems to me that our most pressing problem is how far we have failed as an education system, and more broadly as a community, to respond effectively to the needs of minority communities.

In attempting to design and develop a more effective response to the fact of multi-racialism, and hopefully getting that response — initially at least — geared in to the needs of minorities, it seems to me that we've got to change two elements of our current thinking, quickly and drastically. And in one sense at least, I'd like to eradicate two words from the vocabulary of race relations. We'll never achieve that, and I'll in fact be using those words as I go on, but it's the idea behind the words that I'd like to see eradicated. The first is the notion of 'immigrants': 45% of the black community in this country were *born* here. By the end of this century, (and unfortuntely, before any effective educational solutions take place it may well be the year 2000), 65 or 70% of the black and brown communities will have been born here. So schools now are educating black children born in this country, and this is the first idea to put absolutely at the centre of public, political and professional attention. This means that our problem, our need, and our opportunity, is to enable people to grow up as black and British. To enable them to develop with a positive sense of their own worth, and with a sense of their place in this community, because this is the community that they were born into. That's the first idea.

The second idea, a more difficult one to get over, is that, in a sense, one ought to stop talking about 'minorities'. One ought to do this for a very practical reason. There's no doubt that black and brown people make up a very small minority of the total population — something in the region of 4% is probably the best 'guesstimate' one can make of the percentage of the total population that can be identified by their skin colour. Currently about 7% of all births are born to women who are black or brown. This is a small proportion of the total population. However, because of the uneven distribution of black and brown communities, in certain areas they make up a sizeable proportion of the community that teachers must teach, or social workers relate with, or local services provide effective sets of social policies for. Something like 80% of all black and brown people live in about 15% of census enumeration districts. If you look at the City of Bradford, one third of all births are to women born in Pakistan; if you look at Brent or Hackney or Haringey, or a whole range of inner London boroughs, you find also that about a third of all the births are born to women born in the New Commonwealth. In those areas it's still a minority, but a very sizeable one — often the most significant single element of the school population.

We've no longer talking about **immigrants**, we're not talking about **small minorities**, we're talking about large slices of the school — or the potential school — population. Forty per cent of all the births in inner London, were born to women themselves born outside the U.K., 7% of them in Ireland, 23% of them in the New Commonwealth — i.e. black or brown — and 12% in the rest of the world. For the Inner London Education Authority, which is the biggest in the country, the children of migrants will soon represent 40% of the school population. The language of minorities and thinking about small numbers is simply not relevant here. In those areas, the issue of the needs of migrants' children is a crucial education question, and if we miss it or we make a wrong analysis of it, the educational system is not failing a minority, it's failing a very large part of the school community. So, let's stop thinking of 'immigrants' and 'minorities'.

What are the factors that make up a sensible diagnosis of what the educational needs and problems might be? Well, the first point I've already made: minority communities are heavily concentrated in certain areas.

The second factor — no less important — is the fact of disadvantage: that the areas where black and brown people live are amongst the mst disadvantaged in our whole country. When the Department of the Environment analysed the last census and ranked the 12 areas that were highest in an index of social and economic deprivation, 10 of them were the areas of the heaviest minority concentration. When you look at those enumeration districts where 80% of the black and brown communities live, they have three times the over-crowding, and three times the sharing of housing amenities. The black community lives in areas that are run down (they're not run down because they live there, they were run down before they came), but one of the things we've got to add in to any analysis of what needs doing in the schools is the fact that the problems of race and race relations overlap with the problem of poverty. That's the double bind, or the double jeopardy, of minority communities: the issue of colour and culture on the one hand and the issue of poverty on the other. Kelmer Pringle did a study a few years ago in which she tried to find out what proportion of the child population were multipally disadvantaged — for example, came from overcrowded home conditions, or a poor family, or a single parent family, and so forth. She researched how many children had several of these marks against them in terms of their social development and educational potential. She reckoned that something like 6% of all children were multipally disadvantaged. When we did the same sort of study on West Indians in the London area, the figure we got out for West Indians was 18% — three times the figure for the general population. So when one talks about issues of race relations, when one talks about issues of what ought the schools' response to be, it's not just response to race or ethnicity or colour. It is also a response to deprivation, to disadvantage, to poverty, and the educational problem is a mixture of the racial issue and the problem of poverty.

The third element in this diagnosis of what the schools might be doing is obviously the fact of racial hostility, or racial antagonism and race prejudice. This is a fact of life. The schools are in communities, and those communities contain (and therefore the school contains) all sorts of racial and ethnic stereotypes, and all sorts of racial hostility. That, it seems to me, has got to be registered. It's already registered as a political fact, because clearly it's a major constraint on how far a teacher, or a school, or an education authority are willing to go towards genuinely mobilizing sufficient relevant resources to meet the varied needs of minority communities, and especially those needs that stem from social disadvantage as well as the racial issues.

TABLE I: The percentage of immigrant children fully educated in the U.K. in the top 25% of transfer to Secondary School.

	Verbal Reasoning	English	Mathematics
1966	12	13	14
1968	10	12	12
1971	13	12	12

In some senses schools ought to be most sensitive to the fourth fact in this diagnosis of need: the fact of under-achievement in school as measured by conventional standards. Table I illustrates this under-achievement. The point I want to register here, and very firmly, is that on tests of basic skills, we now have strong evidence to indicate that the performance of children from minority backgrounds is below that of the indigenous children. The most graphic illustration I can give you comes probably at the age of transfer to secondary school. Black and brown children are performing at least a year below the age of their white classmates. This means that instead of functioning at a reading age of 11, they'll be functioning at a reading age of 10. This point can be taken further by not just looking at reading, but looking at the broad spectrum of basic skills contained in the primary school curriculum — namely verbal reasoning, mathematics and English. Now the Inner London Education Authority, at the point of transfer of children to secondary schools, divides them into a top quarter — a top 25% — and a bottom 25%, and a middle 50%. What you'd expect if performance was equal to all groups is that 25% of Asians and 25% of West Indians and 25% of the indigenous would be in the top 25%, and 25% of each group in the bottom 25%. The table divides them in two important ways: by the subject — verbal reasoning, English and mathematics — and by year of transfer — 1966, 1968 and 1971. This is important because obviously one might anticipate some improvement through time. What do we find? By looking at the top 25%, we find that the chances of a black or a brown child, fully educated in this country, being classified in the top 25% in terms of mathematics performance or English performance or verbal reasoning, is roughly half. About 10/12% of them fall in the top 25% and that percentage has not increased in the five or six years under review. Some may say that five or six years is really not very long. But in the primary school life of a child, it is. It's the equivalent of the whole of its primary schooling. So in this period, whole cohorts have gone through the school, and there's no evidence of any improvement.

It's not just a one year gap in reading. It's underfunctioning in the other aspects of the primary school curriculum, and it's relatively stable over time.

The second point on this comes from looking at different ethnic groups. The two main ethnic groups that we're concerned about in race relations are clearly the Asian community on the one hand, and the West Indian community on the other. Now there are many people who see this distinction to be a very divisive one. They feel we shouldn't talk about West Indians on the one hand and Asians on the other, but talk about the coloured or the black community. Again, there is a lot in that argument. But at the same time, there *are* clear distinctions in how well different groups are functioning in the existing school system.

Table II shows the same sort of analysis — it's an analysis of English, maths and verbal reasoning again, and it's children on transfer to secondary school. But it's children fully educated in this country, not people who are recent arrivals, and it shows the difference between those of West Indian origin at the top, Asian origin at the middle, and the indigenous population at the bottom. Figures for the indigenous population should be 25, 25, 25 — they aren't for a variety of reasons, partly for reasons of the test, and partly for the

TABLE II: Percentage of pupils fully educated in the U.K., placed in the upper quartile on transfer to Secondary School, 1968.

	English	Mathematics	Verbal Reasoning
West Indian origin	9	7	7
Asian origin	19	20	21
Indigenous	25	21	20

nature of the inner London population. But the really interesting comparison is between those of West Indian origin and those of Asian origin. What you find is that Asian children, fully educated in London primary schools, are functioning as a group at roughly the same level as the indigenous children, while the West Indian children are not. If you compare the Asian with the indigenous in terms of maths or verbal reasoning, the figures are remarkably similar. But if you look at West Indian children as a group, they are still grossly underfunctioning, and in certain respects this is the most important educational question we should be asking ourselves. Why is it that by the end of the 1960s Asian children were functioning at a roughly similar level in basic skill acquisition to the indigenous, whereas the West Indians were not?

Now I think there are two quite separate reasons that we need to consider in answering that question. The first is contained in how responsive the school or the educational system has been to the different needs of different communities. And the second lies in some characteristics of the communities themselves, what the children bring to school. In other words, the difference between what they receive there and what they bring. In terms of what they receive, it seems to me that the educational system has not found it difficult to identify the crucial, immediate need of the Asian child — namely English as a second language. It's obvious to the school, the teachers, and the community at large, and it's obvious to the politicians. When the National Foundation for Educational Research reviewed policies in multi-racial education, it found that the one set of policies that was clearly being developed throughout the country, was English as a second language — sometimes in special centres, sometimes within individual schools. There was a lot of activity, at least as far as the initial stages of English as a second language were concerned. In a sense, it's the ideal administrative problem; it's fairly simple to identity; we can think of a fairly cheap solution to it; it's relatively effective; and nobody is going to criticise you for doing it.

It seems to me that the West Indian issue is very different, and in so far as we've failed to respond to the needs of the child from a West Indian background, it's because the problem is not as clear-cut and the solutions are not as obvious. In so far as there are solutions, they are not as cheap as English as a second language. On top of this, they are much more threatening, because very often the issue lies in **us,** the majority community, in our attitudes, our feelings, our views about colour and how we react to colour, and how we perceive black communities. Therefore I believe we find it more difficult to respond to the needs of West Indian children. We find them more difficult to diagnose, and in so far as we've got a diagnosis, it is more threatening. People do not like to be told that they are prejudiced or that they discriminate, because it implies the change has got to come in **us.**

Now the second part of this analysis is what the child brings to school. What the **Asian** child brings to school is in a very real sense an alternative culture, an alternative identity, an alternative sense and source of personal well-being and personal strength, to the majority culture. In so far as the majority community or its institutions — the school, the teacher, or the playground — threatens the Asian youngster, they can withdraw: both geographically, into their own community, and also psychologically, into their own sense of personal worth and well-being. They know they are different: they have a different language, a different religion, a different culture and a different set of attitudes, which to no small extent they think is better. And their response to indifference or to ethnic or racial hostility is less to questin their own ethnic identity, than to be pushed back into that sense of identity and well-being, and to derive strength from that.

The West Indian is not in that position. Although there are dangers in pushing this argument too far, the position of the black West Indian is similar to that of the American black. His position represents a variant on the dominant culture, and the dominant culture is rejecting, and therefore there's a danger of community rejection being transferred to self-rejection. There is no religion, no language, no different set of values to fall back on, there is less sense of cultural separateness as a minority.

The most worrying figure in my judgement about performance is contained in Table III. This table compares not Asians with West Indians, and not West Indians with all the indigenous population, but the West Indian with the poorer section of the white community. Now for a long time teachers, professionals, practitioners and the community at large, have been very worried about the under-functioning of the lower working class. We've had Newsome, Crowther, and Plowden as public reports — all concerned about the fact that we are letting down the children who come from working class or semi or unskilled working class backgrounds.

This table is of reading scores: the national mean for a group should be a hundred, and scores out of the same group of children aged 8, 11 (i.e. early

62

TABLE III: London: Reading Test Scores at 8, 11 and 15.
(National mean = 100)

	All children of West Indian origin	West Indians fully educated in UK	White children from unskilled homes
1968 (aged 8)	87.9	89.9	93.7
1971 (aged 11)	87.4	88.7	93.5
1975 (aged 15)	85.9	87.1	92.1

in junior schooling and at the end of primary schooling) and 15 (towards the end of secondary schooling). These figures are all of children fully educated in this country. If you look at all children of West Indian origin and compare them with West Indians fully educated here then those fully educated here are doing rather better. If, however, you compare the West Indians fully educated here with white children from unskilled home backgrounds, you find that the white children at the age of 8 are functioning, as a group, four or five points (which is about 6-months reading age) better. Now remember these are the groups to which a lot of educational thinking has been directed. Yet the black child, fully educated here, at the age of 8, is doing significantly worse than his poor white class-mate. If you look at the age they'd reached in 1971, towards the end of primary schooling, or just before school leaving, the gap is much he same. In fact it is slightly wider at the end of secondary schooling. We are confronted then by a situation which has two elements. One element is a gap between black and poor whites, and the second is a gap which is stable through time. Now I think these are the most disturbing educational findings. It's not just that we're letting down children from the black community, but their performance at schools is on a lower level than the performance of sections of the majority community we've been concerned about for a good many years.

The final part of this diagnosis is the fact of discrimination. The education system in general, and the school in particular, neglects this at its peril. The first reason for saying this is that the school is having to respond to the consequences of discrimination outside it. The earlier experience of many black or brown children has been less good than their parents, or indeed the community at large, might want, simply because of discrimination. Their parents have inferior jobs, they're in inferior housing and things like this affect the child's development. Now when you add on to that the consequences of colonial history and of slavery — in other words the history of race relations — then present issues, needs and problems are partly a result of that. It's nothing to do with school here and now, but the school is having to respond to children whose opportunities and development have been influenced and inhibited because of both current and historical discrimination.

The second thing is that the children themselves are exposed to discrimination and prejudice. One Government inquiry has shown that when you compare white youngsters with black youngsters fully educated here (matched for age, school performance, job aspirations, and for what the teachers expect them to do in the world of work) we still find it takes four times as many interviews with the careers officer to place the black child than the white. Employers clearly still discriminate heavily against black children. So that's a fact the school has got to take note of. It's not of the school's making, but it has got to respond to it and to some extent the school has got to prepare the child to meet it.

In addition, there is prejudice and discrimination within the school itself. *New Society* a few weeks ago published an article that suggested that 25% of adolescents in two boroughs of the East End of London were active supporters of the National Front. Now they didn't become active supporters of the National Front when they left school. The sort of attitudes, beliefs and stereotypes that led them to support the National Front were all and in the classroom the black and the brown child is exposed to it. Furthermore, there's a lot of research to suggest they're exposed to it very young. One particular piece of work was suggesting that at the age of 5 certainly, and maybe even before that, racial stereotypes are already found amongst children.

Equally, the curriculum itself can be accused of being discriminatory, in so far as it has failed to see and to respond to a mixed racial or ethnic community. To no small extent, the curriculum of our schools is still heavily white, anglo-saxon and also protestant. But a large part of the school community is no longer white, it is not anglo-saxon, and not protestant. Now that it is not due to any deliberate conscious decision by the school, but their lack of responsiveness and sensitivity to this one can call, in a sense, passive discrimination.

Perhaps the most difficult fact for the teaching profession to handle is that teachers themselves may reflect some of the attitudes and beliefs found in the wide community. They too may be prejudiced and may actively discriminate. They may have lower expectations for a black youngster. The worrying thing about publicising some of these findings I've been talking about is that they may reinforce some people's expectations. But the fact is that many teachers have lower expectations of black children than white children.

An interesting study was done by the National Foundation for Educational Research asking a group of teachers how they respond to certain questions about children from different backgrounds. The teachers as a group saw West Indian children as being 'stupid' and being 'trouble makers' — very clear negative stereotypes.

In so far as these stereotypes exist and are communicated to black children, they will be factors in the children's responsiveness to the school, their attitudes to school, and their own views and images of themselves — all the things that teachers professionally know are profoundly important in determining how well or how badly a child does.

What have I been trying to argue? That the centre of our attention ought to be the special needs of black and brown children in our schools. That in fact the school has a responsibility, and has a potentiality for doing something about these special needs, which has been fully accepted politically. What is less accepted is how to translate this into effective action. It seems to me that, professionally speaking, teachers need to give up thinking about 'immigrants' and give up thinking about 'minorities'. We should think in terms of black Britons, and black Britons in large numbers and in high proportions in some parts of our cities and in many of our schools. Until we accept that message I don't think we're going to get very far.

Further, we have got to accept the point that we are not performing very well at the moment. There is clear evidence that, as far as at least the West Indian community is concerned, there is a gross and disturbing under-functioning.

This is worrying for two reasons. First, the education system is missing an opportunity to meet the genuine and legitimate needs of pupils. And second, it is no less worring that if we continue to miss this opportunity we may be sowing the seeds for racial disharmony and racial discontent, and certainly reinforcing racial injustice. We may well be producing situations in which young black people leave school unemployed and unemployable. Wasted opportunities mean wasted lives; without justice between groups, harmony is a fiction. Without special educational effort neither justice nor harmony can be achieved; that is both the educational challenge and the warning.

Third World Perspective: Bishop Trevor Huddleston
Bishop of Stepney 1968-78

Bishop Huddleston gave this lecture a few days before leaving Stepney to become Bishop of Mauritius. His diocese included the London Boroughs of Tower Hamlets, Hackney and Islington, where there are substantial Bangladeshi and West Indian communities. Before commencing his lecture, Bishop Huddleston reflected that when he arrived in Stepney the Asian community was demanding more effective police protection against the 'paki-bashers', many of whom were identified as skinheads. Ten years later, on the eve of his departure, the problem of assaults against Asians still persisted, on an even greater scale.

On the corner of Brick Lane and Fournier Street at the Whitechapel end of Stepney, there stands a very noble building. It has stood there since 1743, when the great wave of Hugenot refugees settled in Spitalfields and set up their silk weaving industry — incidentally planting Mulberry trees for the silk worms all over the East End, one of which I have in my back yard. Those first immigrants prospered and moved into the wider community and became part of it. Not before, through their own industry, integrity and originality in the clothing trade, they had made a massive contribution to the commercial life of our city.

But they were succeeded, as they moved away from the East End, by another much larger, much poorer wave of immigrants who sailed up the river, this time refugees from the pogroms of Poland and Tsarist Russia. They came and settled in the same area, but by the time they settled there the green fields, open spaces and rather handsome houses and squares that the Hugenots had known had been replaced by desperately overcrowded backyards and by dark and forbidding tenement buildings. This was about 1898. And they perforce, because of their extreme poverty, had to find somewhere to live in that desperately overcrowded scene. Moreover, they had not only to find somewhere to live, they had to find a trade which would make it possible for them to live — and they did so. They, as we all know, established the clothing industry in a rather different form from their predecessors, and again by hard work, by tremendous industry and initiative were able to establish themselves there in that same place. And being what they were, they needed somewhere to worship God.

And so, very soon after their arrival they found the Huguenot Chapel, bought it and converted it into the Great Synagogue. And that synagogue was in full use until six years ago. That Jewish immigration had a vast impact, not only on the East End of London, not only on London itself but on the whole nation. I dare to say that that immigration, at every level of our life, has enriched us more than any other. One of its greatest riches was a poet who walked the streets of Stepney penniless for years, and in the end when the Great War broke out joined up. In his own account of things, he joined up in order simply to get at least a living as well as to serve in the only way he could his adopted country. Isaac Rosenberg — one of the many of those Jewish immigrants whose contribution to the culture of our land has been without price.

I want to just read a few lines of his, because I think they're relevant to our theme, it's a poem called 'The Jew'.

Moses, from whose loins I sprung
Lit by a lamp in his blood
Ten immutable rules
A moon for mutable lampless men
The blond, the bronze, the ruddy
With the same heaving blood keep tide
To the moon of Moses
Then why do they sneer at me?

The Great Synagogue was, of course, the focus and centre for the Jewish immigrant community of Spitalfields for nearly a century. A marvellous place, redolent of the history of the East End. But then that community also moved out into the wider community, having itself made this massive contribution at every level of our life, until there were too few to use the synagogue — a quorum could no longer be found. In 1975 the Great Synagogue was sold. It was sold to another community of immigrants, this time the Bengali community from Bangladesh — devout Muslims — and it has become the Great Mosque.

So you see, that building in Brick Lane is a kind of symbol of what it means to live at the point of arrival for immigrant communities in our country. And I can't think of a more impressive or more meaningful symbol.

That the mosque has been, in turn, a Christian church and a Jewish synagogue is symbolic of more than that alone. Hugenots were the victims of religious persecution at a time when Europe was still fighting through the consequences of the Renaissance and the Reformation. Jews, as so often in their history, were the victims of racial persecution, but in the case of that particular wave of immigrants, many were anarchists and some were great ones — Jews who fled to Britain persecuted not only for their race but for political idealism, supposedly disruptive of the society from which they came.

Bengalis from East Pakistan (or Bangladesh) are not refugees from persecution — religious, racial or political. They are refugees from poverty and they are representatives in Britain of what we have learnt to call the Third World. But they are also representatives of what I would call the entail of history — our history. They are directly the consequence of emigration — of those who used the river not as a point of arrival but as a point of departure. First in wooden ships as explorers, then in much larger vessels as colonists, moving out and away by their thousands into the countries that they colonised and conquered and ruled for so many years. I believe most passionately that unless we are prepared to understand and recognise this entail of history — not just in words, and certainly not just as a fact in the history book — then we cannot hope to begin to understand the meaning either of race relations in our land, or of that element in race relations which is now the focus of attention for politicians and the media which we call immigration.

I'm glad to quote tonight, in his presence, a sentence from the report on British race relations of nearly a decade ago, edited by one of the most distinguished of the Runnymede trustees — Mr Jim Rose, who said this in the most significant report that has ever been produced on the subject: *'the dominant question of our century is whether men of all races and colours whom advance in science and technology have made near neighbours can live together in harmony'*. It's precisely because I believe this statement to be true that I can view the issue of race relations in our country as transcending every other issue at this time, and that I can view it only in one context. Obviously, all of us has his own life time of experience behind him, which has shaped and moulded his ideas much more than he's aware. As it happens, I have had two widely contrasting experiences: one in South Africa at the very beginning of the legislative process which has imposed Apartheid with ever more stringent sanctions and more appalling consequences over the past 30 years — and Soweto was part of my parish — so I have known racism, as you might say, at its fountain head. I've also had experience of living in a country at the moment of transition from colonialism to freedom — a Third World country, a poor country, one of the poorest in fact in the Commonwealth. I've lived there for eight years in one of its poorest regions, at grass roots, with the problems of Third World hunger and development. Therefore, naturally, the only way in which I can perceive for myself the meaning of the issue of race relations is from the point of arrival for me at the end of those years. It is because immigration and our treatment of immigrant communities has become the immediate test of this far wider issue, that it is significant.

Mr Ronald Butt, in an article in *The Times,* a few weeks ago, said, I quote: *'for many who do not think themselves cut off from Christian morality, there is a question which perhaps does not trouble Bishop Huddleston: what rights should be allowed to a civilised people who wish to preserve what they see as their identity by placing restrictions on people from other countries and nations who wish to come to their country to work?'*

I need hardly say here that that question does in fact trouble me a great deal, though perhaps for rather different reasons from those which concern Mr Butt. Certainly for different reasons also from those which concern, or seem

68

to concern, the leader of one of our two main political parties. And in his own idiosyncratic way, Mr Enoch Powell. It bothers me precisely because I believe that unless the false perspective created by the numbers game and the kind of arguments used in playing it can be changed, unless the mass media can be persuaded to eliminate bias in favour of integrity, and pandering to prejudice in favour of responsible and educative assessment, then I would say the future is very bleak indeed.

The greatest danger, as I see it, to an effective initiative from any quarter concerning the problems and opportunities of immigrant communities is the bland assumption that such an initiative can be taken to isolation from the world-wide context. It isn't only of course that immigrants come from somewhere, and that somewhere is, in the case of all of those who settle in Britain, part of the Commonwealth, new or old. It's also that their treatment, the racial attitudes evoked by their presence, the political reactions of governments and individuals in an age of mass communications has an immediate and sometimes far-reaching effect on race relations — not in this land alone, but thoughout the world. After all, as long ago as 1903, W.E.B. Dubois, the American writer, could say the problem of the 20th century is the problem of the colour line. The relation of the darker to the lighter races of men in Asia, in Africa, in America, and he said prophetically, "the islands of the sea". He didn't define those islands, but I would. For me, we stand on one of the islands of the sea quite directly and explicitly involved in this problem, in this issue, in this opportunity. What is really new about it can be stated quite simply and without qualification — it is that it has passed from being a local problem, or a series of local problems, to being inescapably a world problem. It has become this not in the minds of a few thinkers like Dubois, but in reality for five distinct but related reasons.

First, because whether we like it or not, instant communication by satellite, television and radio have made it so — we wear mankind as our skin. This fact of instant communication means not only that we're present with events as they happen, but also that a speech delivered to a local audience — let us say in Birmingham or Bradford or Wolverhampton — has an immediate impact in Dar-es-Salaam or New Delhi or Pretoria.

Secondly, because the past twenty years have seen a colossal shift of power on the great continents and sub-continents of Africa and Asia and a new world has come into being to redress the balance of the old. Hundreds of millions of people of this planet earth have experienced liberation — at least political liberation — within the context of emergent nationhood. Those who've experienced this liberation have been of a different colour from their former rulers. They have experienced, alongside that liberation, all the traumas that beset any nation at its point of discovering its own identity.

Thirdly, this has happened at a moment in history when political freedom, as we well know, is a fragile thing at best, and is by no means to be identified with economic or cultural freedom. The consequences of this factor for both the developing and the developed nations and more especially for our own, is immeasurable but immense. To quote one of the more prophetic voices of our day — President Julius Nyerere — speaking on his own land: *'Our poverty, our ignorance and our disease are not an inevitable part of the human condition. Once we accepted these things as the will of God, now they are recognised as being within the control of man. Political freedom is therefore no longer enough for us, we are determined to maintain our mastery over our own destiny — to defend our national freedom. We are also determined to change the condition of our lives.'*

The facts of world poverty and world hunger, the consequences of population explosion — all of us are aware that these are the basic challenges confronting our generation if we see it from a world perspective. Unless we can do this, then inescapably the kind of decision-making that we go in for with regard to the issue of race relations in our own land is bound to be misguided and will lead inescapably to disaster. What has to be brought home to people immediately is the fact that the affluent and the hungry world stand today basically on opposite sides of a colour line. The fact itself isn't new, its dimensions and its inescapability are — and the gulf is widening. Whether we like it or not, we are all involved in its consequences and nowhere more than at this particular moment in time, when because of the movement of peoples, because of what we call immigration or emigration, we here in this land are caught up in the process. It will not be changed in its final and perhaps wholly disastrous result by repatriation, by the use of entry permits, by the forcible exclusion of people because they do not fall into a particular category of family relationships, or the fact that their particular culture and way of life is alien to that of the local host community.

The ideological division of our world is the fourth issue with which we have to live, a powerfully divisive factor, though now subject to changing, new forms. Ideologically speaking, East and West are no longer — if they ever were — monolithic. It's impossible to say that the Communist world or the Capitalist world, or however you define these things, are so structured that no change can or will occur in their attitudes to one another. But the ideologies are still immensely strong, and ideological conflict on the local scene, between right and left, between National Front and Socialist Workers Party, are but reflections of something which is there within the context of the world scene.

And finally, the issue of racialism has moved from being a local to a world issue for a reason rather harder to define, but certainly as important in its implications as the four I've already listed. There is no question that the most powerful force in the Third World today is national cultural awareness. Of course it must be, at this moment when the new countries are discovering the meaning of nationhood and their own identity as nations. Nationalism in this sense is a positive and constructive force — the force in fact which builds or creates a nation. Anyone who's lived in a newly independent state will recognise that far more than ideology, more than religion, more than politics in its restrictive sense, this is the attractive and unitive power, especially for those who are building the nations. And yet the very phrase — the Third World — hints at a conflict of ideals. For whilst it's true that the first priority must be national identity and freedom, it's also true that this can only be achieved and safeguarded by international relationships. The military and economic elements operative in the building of new nations compel them to seek a wider community somewhere. Their vulnerability over against the great power blocks of east and west compels them to seek some kind of security or some way of moving out into greater freedom. The tragedy of this is, of course, that this particular element in development militates against solving the problems of development because it compels nations to concentrate so much of their resources on armaments and destructive weapons.

Nevertheless this world, the Third World, however shadowy and indefinable the phrase is sometimes — is a growing reality, with enormous potential for the future. It is a coloured world, and a part of it, a very small part numerically speaking, is now a part of Britain's plural society.

The immigrant communities from the West Indies, Pakistan, India, East Africa are, of course, involved in this moment of transition. Thousands of the children in our schools, thousands of those children who've left our schools for the labour market or the dole queue, born in our country knowing no other, are nevertheless in a sense the representatives of this world. And like us, they are also part of the international order to which we all belong — the world in which we have to create a new kind of patriotism if we are to survive.

A great question mark hangs over the future of the immigrant communities of course, because by the accident of history they have to live in areas of multiple deprivation. They have to accept educational facilities which are already inadequate. They have to find somewhere in which to build up their families in conditions which are socially disruptive from the very start. Of course a great insecurity hangs around them, but don't let us delude ourselves into imagining that it doesn't also hang over the rest of us in Britain and our future too. They may be, indeed they are, small communities by comparison with a population of 55 million. Even where they appear to be a large population because they find themselves in the 'ghetto' areas of our cities and are forced to stay there because of housing shortages and economic problems connected with job opportunities, they are still minority groups. But Great Britain is also itself a small community over against the world from which the immigrant communities have come.

Philip Mason in his book *Patterns of Dominance*[1] makes a valuable distinction between what he describes as two ideals of society, seldom explicitly stated by either party, clear and quite distinct. One pictures a nation state, homogeneous in language and custom; the other, a new kind of society in which there is believed to be equal opportunity for all, but in which there is a diversity of language and culture, various groups of varied origin keeping their distinctive nature and enriching the whole by their contribution. The two views differ in other ways. Those who picture a homogeneous nation state are usually much more reconciled to class differences, while those who value cultural diversity are generally hostile to class. The latter see the world as an industrial city to which the countryside is a playground, while the former often romanticise a rural scene that is disappearing. But the important difference is between homogeneity and diversity. There are indications, (Mason was writing quite a few years back), that at present the considerable majority of Englishmen still think of the homogeneous nation state as their ideal.

Which, in fact, of these two views is more truly compatible with a sane view of race relations in the kind of world, in which, whether we like it or not, we live? Which is more compatible with a future for a nation such as ours, totally dependent upon trade and commerce with the world, and totally dependent for its survival and certainly for the survival of reasonable living standards, upon the products of that world? What is it at this present turning point in human history, symbolized perhaps by man's venture into space, and the concept of one world which I've tried to give you, that hinders or even totally prevents a sane view, a common mind and common action on this issue?

Clearly there's room for argument and for genuine difference of opinion as there's been all through history, on the kind of social structure or society in which man can most completely be free to develop his own potential. But there are limits and boundaries within every society which are there whether we like it or not. It is not likely that this argument is going to end very neatly or very soon, but certainly the logic of the present situation seems to me to be inescapable. The one world to which we all belong and the inter-related problems of survival which have arisen as the result of human inventiveness, scientific and technological mastery, is a world in which men of different race, colour and creed must, in the words of W. H. Auden — love one another or die.

But to turn this message into practical reality is the challenge to our generation, and is I believe peculiarly the challenge to our country because of the entail of history which is ours.

It may be true that we have lost an empire and not discovered a role. It is also true that no nation on earth has had such wide, vast and extensive influence on other nations in this past century, by reason of its colonial policies and its government of great sections of the continents of the earth. No nation, therefore, has had such wide or such recent experience of close relationships with the peoples of Africa and Asia and the Caribbean. And perhaps also, though this still remains to be seen, history cannot show another example in which on the whole, the relinquishment of power, the end of colonialism, has given us such marvellous opportunities of making a positive and real contribution to the future.

The fact, or rather the recognition of the fact, that we live in a plural society in any case, and that this is a desirable thing in itself, means a recognition of the fact that society is enriched by the presence of different cultural groups and by their diversity. It's also recognition of the stimulus that such a society must provide towards mutual tolerance and understanding.

So, in conclusion, I ask what are the enemies of effective action in this field of race relations in our country today? I think they are not hard to identify. First, there is a profound ignorance, amongst even intelligent citizens, of the issues involved. Whether considered universally or locally, the peculiar paradox of our generation is the fact that through the mass media we are receiving far more information about the world than we can digest, and therefore the use of generalities in our reference to the problems and opportunities presented to us, is something which in itself is destructive. It's far easier to speak of 'immigrants' or 'immigration' than to define this in particular terms.

Following from this, though perhaps not always connected with it, there is a profound insensitivity in the corridors of power to the reality and meaning of the problem. It's almost as if sometimes those who are in authority in Government lose the imagination and the insight that they must have if they are to recognise the true significance of the era in which we live.

Thirdly, and I believe one of the greatest enemies, is sloth — again no doubt encouraged by the use of mass media. Intellectual sloth, a kind of moral turpitude, in really taking the trouble to come to grips with the basic issues confronting the local community. It's so much easier to accept what you see and hear on television than to think about it and act from sane conclusions. Professor Banton wrote that one of the tendencies that does most to hinder the understanding of race relations is to seek for explanations in terms of a single factor. For instance, the inclination of some people to maintain that racial friction is caused by instinct, custom, exploitation, etc. As if, say, inflation in an economic system could be explained as caused only by human greediness. In this matter perhaps more than any other, we have to discipline ourselves to ask the right questions.

I believe that our society doesn't, in fact, place much value on such self-discipline.

Then there's our obsessive mood with a need to see everything in terms of economic solutions. The need to take our economic temperature twenty times a day to be certain that we're still alive, and the dire consequences of making this the yardstick for all human affairs.

How on earth are we going to do the things that must be done swiftly, within the inner-city areas of our land, to meet the problems of existing deprivation which is the basic problem in race relations for thousands upon thousands of our own people and of those who live in these areas? How are we going to do this if our priority continues to be driven increasingly in the direction of providing more things — what we call sustaining and increasing our standard of living?

Well, I believe that behind all these other enemies lurks the greatest enemy of all — fear. Because the origins of racial friction lie so deep, because prejudice and the discrimination resulting from it have such irrational forces mixed up with them, we dare not examine them honestly. Rationalisation substitutes for seeking the remedies. We use the kind of language which will disguise from ourselves the reality of what we're saying.

You mean, for instance, apartheid, segregation. But if you're a white South African you call it 'separate development'. You mean discrimination and you call it 'the encouragement of indigenous culture'. You mean white supremacy and you call it the 'safeguarding of Christian civilization'. There's virtually no limit to human ingenuity when it comes to pushing away its fears. You use statistics to prove your rationality.

Fear, which drives you to identify alleged danger as alien, and immediately you have your scapegoat for the many present ills of our over-crowded city centres with their housing shortages, inadequate educational facilities, lack of playground space and all the rest. You refuse the attempt at an appeal to tolerance and appeal instead to the stronger instinct of self-preservation. You aim at eliminating the alien presence, which in fact means your own fellow men, by removing it from sight. Whether, as Mr Powell suggests, by repatriation, or whether, as the South African government does, by an enforced segregation which prevents all social contact between human beings. But you do all these things and provide all the necessary rationalisation for your actions because in fact you are afraid.

Some of you may remember a moment in that great novel of Alan Paton's, written a generation ago — *Cry the Beloved Country,* in which a black priest is talking to his white friend, a South African, about this common, tragic predicament. He says, *"I have one great fear in my heart that when they are turned to loving we shall be turned to hating".*

Racism, wrote Martin Luther King, is a philosophy based on a contempt for life. I believe that to be true because I've seen the working out of that philosophy in South Africa. You've seen it too if you've lived through the Second World War — in Auschwitz, and Belsen and Buchenwald. Racism is total estrangement, and I believe this to be true also, for I've experienced the effects of that estrangement in an apartheid society. And alas, much nearer home. You've experienced it also if you've known at first hand the loneliness and vulnerability of the immigrant in a great city, and I have known that too.

Are we capable, at this crisis point in history, of fulfilling our role — whatever it costs, whoever we are, whatever else we do? Over twenty years ago I wrote a book about my experiences in South Africa, and I chose the title from a poem by G. K. Chesterton — *'I tell you nought for your comfort, yea nought for your desire, save that the sky grows darker yet, and the sea rises higher'*. But the poem continues — *'night shall be thrice night over you, and heaven an iron cope, but do you have joy without a cause, or faith without a hope'*.

Reference
[1]Published by Oxford University Press 1970.

A note on obtaining this book, and BBC films, and other materials on race relations

Race Relations and Employment

The Commission for Racial Equality offers tutors, trainers and discussion group leaders a one third discount on orders for six copies or more of this book, which has been made with the hope that they will want to supply it as course material.

The five Multi-Racial Britain programmes are being shown again at least twice by BBC Television in the same order as in this book. First, on Mondays at 10.30 a.m. on BBC2, starting on 8 January 1979. This showing is specifically for ease of off-air recording in educational institutions, for subsequent use of the films as teaching or training aids and as stimulus to discussion groups.

Second, on Sundays at 11.50 a.m. on BBC1, starting 18 March 1979. (The last talk on 15 April will be at 12.35 p.m.) Discussion group leaders who do not have access to off-air recording machines are asked to help draw attention to these transmissions, which lead up to a new series of ten documentary training and educational films about ways of improving race relations at the local community level, which are planned to be first shown on BBC1 on Tuesdays, at 11.15 p.m., starting on 24 April 1979. (While the five public talks offer an introductory analysis of the race relations issues, the follow-up set of training films go on to review some of the possible practical solutions.)

For details of further repeat transmissions of all those programmes in 1979 and 1980, contact BBC Education Broadcasting Information, (30/RM/FE), BBC, London W1A 1AA (01-580 4468, ext 3229.)

In selecting just five talks for the BBC series, perhaps the most important aspect of race relations that we've not covered is the field of race and employment. This is partly because the BBC Further Education Department has already contributed several programmes to this theme.

The film *Trade Union Studies — Immigrant Workers* sets out the basic figures on the place of West Indians and Asians in Britain's workforce. (Numerically, they in fact make up only a little over 3%. Irish immigrant workers make up over 4%. And the combined total of 7.5% compares with 11% immigrant workers in France and Germany, and no less than 25 to 30% in Switzerland.) The film goes on to review trade union reactions to their black members, drawing attention not only to the need for more industrial language training, but also for equal opportunity clauses in collective bargaining contracts together with monitoring arrangements to ensure that these are effective in practice. Made by trade unionists for discussion by trade unionists, that film is available for hire in 16mm form, from BBC Enterprises, Villiers House, Ealing Broadway, London W5 (01-743 8000 ext 394/5).

In addition there are the four films of the *Worktalk* series. The first, *Asians on the Shop Floor* asses the value of industrial language training, together with sensitivity training of supervisors to the cultural background of Asians, through the eyes of supervisors themselves in factories near Birmingham and near Southall. The second, *Fred Barker goes to China* is a light-hearted film giving vicarious experience of what its like to be an immigrant worker. (This is designed to be especially useful in disarming defensive attitudes in training sessions or discussions of race relations). The third *Singh 171* is a dramatised case study raising issues for managers about the promotion of Asian workers. The fourth, *T'aint what you say, its the way that you say it* ... analyses the commonest communication difficulties in multi-racial workplaces, with practical hints for shop stewards and supervisors in how to cope with them. A detailed *Worktalk* Trainers Manual, essential for fully effective use of the films, is available for £3.00 from The Runnymede Trust, 62 Chandos Place, London WC2 (01-836-3266). The films themselves are on hire, for £4.00 each from Concord Films, 201 Felixstowe Road, Ipswich, Suffolk (Phone: 0473-79300).

The *Worktalk* series is being transmitted by the BBC again at 10.30 am on Tuesdays, on BBC 2, starting 9 January 1979. Again, this is an opportunity for free off-air recording, all for all concerned with better multi-racial understanding to help draw the *Worktalk* series to the attention of industrial trainers, tutors of personnel and supervisors' courses, employers and trade union representatives, both in private industry and in public services.

SELECTED CRE PUBLICATIONS

CONFERENCE REPORT: Strategy Statement and Speeches from the National Conference of CRCs at Leicester **75p**

EDUCATIONAL NEEDS OF CHILDREN FROM MINORITY GROUPS: Reference Series No. 1 . . . . **30p**

THE EDUCATION OF ETHNIC MINORITY CHILDREN **80p**

IN SERVICE EDUCATION OF TEACHERS IN MULTI-RACIAL AREAS: An Evaluation of Current Practice **60p**

A SECOND CHANCE: Further Education in Multi-Racial Areas **£1.35**

MEETING THEIR NEEDS: An Account of Language Tuition Schemes for Ethnic Minority Women **80p**

DON'T RUSH ME: The Comic-Strip, Sex Education and Multi-Racial Society — by Sarah Curtis **35p**

THE EMPLOYMENT OF NON-ENGLISH SPEAKING WORKERS: What Industry Must Do: Ref. Series No. 2 . . . . **50p**

WORLD RELIGIONS: Aids for Teachers (3rd Edition) **£1.50**

UNEMPLOYMENT & HOMELESSNESS: A Report: Reference Series No. 3 (HMSO) **£1.00**

HOUSING IN MULTI-RACIAL AREAS: A Report of a Working Party of Housing Directors **60p**

HOUSING CHOICE AND ETHNIC CONCENTRATION: An Attitude Study **90p**

ETHNIC MINORITIES IN THE INNER CITY: The Ethnic Dimension in Urban Deprivation in England — by Chrispin Cross **£1.80**

URBAN DEPRIVATION, RACIAL INEQUALITY AND SOCIAL POLICY: A Report: Reference Series No. 13 (HMSO) **£1.75**

FOSTERING BLACK CHILDREN: Reference Series No 6 . . . . **30p**

WHO MINDS! A Study of Working Mothers and Childminding in Ethnic Minority Communities **75p**

ASPECTS OF MENTAL HEALTH IN A MULTI-CULTURAL SOCIETY: Refernce Series No. 10 . . . . **60p**

CARING FOR UNDER-FIVES IN A MULTI-RACIAL SOCIETY **60p**

ONE YEAR ON: A Report on the Resettlement of the Refugees from Uganda in Britain: Ref Series No. 4 . . . . **75p**

REFUGE OR HOME?: A Policy Statement on the Resettlement of Refugees: Reference Series No 7 . . . . **75p**

SOME OF MY BEST FRIENDS...: A Report on Race Relations Attitudes: Ref. Series No 8 **45p**

PARTICIPATION OF ETHNIC MINORITIES IN THE GENERAL ELECTION, October 1974. . . . . **45p**

BETWEEN TWO CULTURES: A Study in Relationship between Generations in the Asian Community in Britain: Reference Series No 12 . . . . **£1.00**

THE ARTS BRITAIN IGNORES: The Arts of Ethnic Minorities in Britain — by Naseem Khan **£1.50**

DOCTORS FROM OVERSEAS: A Case for Consultation: Reference Series No. 9 . . . . **50p**

MULTI-RACIAL BRITAIN: The Social Services Response. A report of a Working Party of the Association of directors of social services and the Commission for Racial Equality . . . **£1.00**

MUSLIM BURIALS: A Policy Paper (Reprint) **25p**

AS THEY SEE IT: A Race Relations Study of Three Areas From a Black view-point — by Lionel Morrison: Reference Series No. 11 . . . . **£1.25**

SEEN BUT NOT SERVED: Black Youth & the Youth Service **50p**

MULTI-RACIAL BRITAIN: The Social Services response: A Working Party Report **£1.00**

NO PROBLEMS HERE?: Management and Multi-Racial Workforce including a Guide to the Race Relations Act, 1976 (IPM & CRE) **£1.50**

WHO TUNES IN TO WHAT? A Report on Ethnic Minority Broadcasting — by Muhammad Anwar **£1.20**

RACE AND LAW by Anthony Lester and Geoffrey Bindman.

FIRST REPORT OF THE CRE (June 1977 – December 1977). HMSO.

ASPIRATIONS VERSUS OPPORTUNITIES: Asian and White School-leavers in the Midlands.

ETHNIC MINORITIES IN BRITAIN: Statistical Background.

RACIAL DISCRIMINATION: A Guide to the Race Relations Act, 1976 (prepared by the Home Office).

LOOKING FOR WORK: Black and White School Leavers in Lewisham.

FREE BOOKLETS/LEAFLETS

EQUAL OPPORTUNITY IN EMPLOYMENT: A Guide for Employers.

LOCAL AUTHORITIES AND SECTION 71 OF THE RACE RELATIONS ACT, 1976

MONITORING AN EQUAL OPPORTUNITY POLICY: A Guide for Employers.

A GUIDE TO ASIAN NAMES.

A GUIDE TO THE NEW RACE RELATIONS ACT: Advertisement, Employment, Landlords and Accommodation Agencies.

BOOKS AND PERIODICALS IN ASIAN LANGUAGES.

EVIDENCE TO THE ROYAL COMMISSION ON THE DISTRIBUTION OF INCOME AND WEALTH (CRC).

ETHNIC MINORITIES IN BRITAIN: Statistical Background

FACT SHEETS: 1 Immigration, 2 Housing, 3 Employment.

FACT PAPERS (These papers on race relations were written and compiled for trade union use at the request of the Trade Union Advisory Group of the former CRC): 1 The Basic Figures, 2 Immigration – Numbers and Dispersal, 3 Background of Asian Minority Groups, 4 The Language Barrier in Employment.

FILM CATALOGUE: Community and Race Relations (2nd edition).

LIST OF COMMUNITY RELATIONS COUNCILS.

LIST OF ETHNIC MINORITY PRESS.

PUBLIC LIBRARY SERVICE FOR MULTI-CULTURAL SOCIETY: A Report produced by the Library Advisory Council & the former CRC Education Committee.

RACE RELATIONS IN BRITAIN: A Select Bibliography with Emphasis on Ethnic Minorities (7th edition).

SOME PEOPLE WILL BELIEVE ANYTHING: Myths and Facts About Immigration and Race Relations.

STRATEGY STATEMENT: A Programme for Action. Also available in: Bengali, Gujarati, Hindi, Punjabi, Urdu.

THE MULTI-RACIAL COMMUNITY: A Guide for Local Councillors.

TRAINING GRANTS AND SUBSIDIES: A Guide to Government Initiative on Employment.

YOUR RIGHTS TO EQUAL TREATMENT UNDER THE NEW RACE RELATIONS ACT 1976: A General Guide, Employment, Housing, Education and Services.
Poster: Know Your Rights (Available in English, Bengali, Gujarati, Hindi, Punjabi and Urdu).

A BIBLIOGRAPHY FOR TEACHERS (4th edition)

AUDIO-VISUAL AIDS FOR TEACHERS.

BOOKS FOR UNDER-FIVES IN MULTI-RACIAL BRITAIN.

DIALECT IN SCHOOL – by J. Wight (Reprint from *Education Review* Vol. 24 No. 1).

EDUCATION OF ETHNIC MINORITIES: CRE's Comments on the Consultative Document issued by the D.E.S. on the Report on the West Indian Community by the Select Committee on Race Relations and Immigration. Occasional Paper No. 1.

EVIDENCE ON EDUCATION TO THE SELECT COMMITTEE: Enquiry on the West Indian Community (CRC November 1976).

LANGUAGE – by Christopher Candlin and June Derrick (2nd edition).

SCHOOLS AND ETHNIC MINORITIES: CRE's Comments on 'Education in Schools: A Consultative Document' issued by the D.E.S. Occasional Paper No. 3.

TEACHER EDUCATION FOR A MULTI-CULTURAL SOCIETY: Report of a Joint Working Party of the CRC and ATCD.

YOUNG TONGUES EXTENDED: A Handbook for Pre-school Language Groups — by Judith Lillie.

ESTATE AGENTS AND RACIAL DISCRIMINATION: A Summary of Evidence.

HOUSING AND COMMUNICATION WITH ETHNIC MINORITIES: Report of a one-day Seminar for London Housing Aid Centre Managers (20 May 1975).

HOUSING NEED AMONG ETHNIC MINORITIES: CRE's Comment on the Consultative Document on Housing Policy presented to Parliament by the Secretary of State for Environment and the Secretary of State for Wales. Occasional Paper No. 2.

HOUSING CENTRES AND THE ASIAN COMMUNITY by Michael Pettit.

JOINT MORTGAGES: A Discussion Paper.

RESEARCH SUMMARIES:
  COLOUR AND REHOUSING: A Study of Redevelopment in Leeds by Christopher Duke.
  CONSTRAINTS ON IMMIGRANT HOUSING CHOICE: Estate Agents by Stuart Hatch.
  RACE AND COUNCIL HOUSING IN LONDON by David Smith (PEP 1975).

ACCIDENTS ARE COLOUR-BLIND: Industrial Accidents and the Immigrant Worker.

AFRO HAIR AND SKIN CARE: Some Basic Information.

A HOME FROM HOME?: Some Policy Consideraiton of Black Children in Residential Care.

A GUIDE TO ASIAN DIETS: A Background Paper.

CHILD BENEFIT — BUT NOT FOR ALL?: Comments on the Child Benefit Scheme. Occasional Paper No. 4.

MENTAL HEALTH AMONG MINORITY ETHNIC GROUPS: Research Summaries and Bibliography.

RESEARCH SUMMARIES ON THE UNDER-FIVES.

RICKETS AND ANAEMIA: Report of a Conference held on 5 December 1974.

SICKLE CELL ANAEMIA.

SOCIAL WORK TRAINING IN A MULTI-RACIAL SOCIETY: A Course for Tutors, Lecturers on CQSW Courses, Practice Teachers and Student Unit Supervisors.

THE VIEW OF SOCIAL WORKERS IN MULTI-RACIAL AREAS.

TRAINING NURSERY NURSES FOR A MULTI-RACIAL COMMUNITY: Report of a Seminar for NNEB Tutors held in February 1976.

WORKING IN MULTI-RACIAL AREAS: A Training Handbook for Social Services Departments.

PERIODICALS

NEW COMMUNITY — Quarterly: £1.75 per copy as from Vol. VII
(Index to vols 1, 2, 3 & 4 at 50p each)

EDUCATION JOURNAL (6 issues a year).

EMPLOYMENT REPORT (4 issues a year)

NETWORK (6 issues a year).

KING ALFRED'S COLLEGE

LIBRARY